Stop Smoking Script
Pre-talk & Hypnosis
Psychotherapy & Hypnotherapy
Neuro-Linguistic Programming (NLP)
Cognitive Behavioural Therapy (CBT)
Clinical Psychology

By
David Glenn

I am dedicating this book to my clients, in appreciation.
Thank you, because without you I would never have had the experience,
and therefore the knowledge, to write this book.
David Glenn.

Stop Smoking Script Pre-talk & Hypnosis Psychotherapy & Hypnotherapy - 2

Copyright 2008 – Revised May 2017 - David Glenn.
All rights reserved. No Unauthorized copying, distribution or use as a teaching aid.

Disclaimer, Legal Warning and Notice

THE INFORMATION ENCLOSED is for the use of the person who purchased it for reading purposes only. In spite of that, if you so wish, the knowledge can be used on yourself or clients at your own discretion. You do not have permission to resell, reprint/copy or retype any of the information enclosed, and it is not for use in teaching any classes with students. Whilst all attempts have been made to verify and check the information in this publication, neither the author, nor the publisher assumes any responsibility for errors, omissions or inaccuracies. All rights reserved. No part of this information may be reproduced or transmitted in any form, or by any means, electronically or mechanically, including, but not limited to photocopying, recording, or any form of information storage or retrieval system, without the written permission from David Glenn.

This information is provided "as is" without warranty of any kind. In no event shall David Glenn be liable for any loss of profits, loss of business, loss of use of data, interruption of business, or for indirect, special, incidental, or consequential damages of any kind, arising from any error or recommendation in this material. By purchasing, or reading this book, you are agreeing and fully understand that you are responsible for your own conduct, now and in the future. The author and publisher take no liability for your actions in any way, shape or form. It is strongly advised that you do not misuse any of the techniques being taught, and we insist that you have legal insurance cover before hypnotising, or carrying therapy out on anyone.

It is with deep regret that a few past students and rival companies have attempted to copy this book and claim it as their own. Putting your name to this book as your own work, or teaching your own classes/students from it, is an infringement of copyright. I must make it clear that I take theft of my material very seriously and legal action is always taken under those circumstances. Once you have read this book and therefore gained my knowledge, I am more than happy for you to earn a good living from the information provided with clients, but not with students teaching. Please respect the years of work that I have done to produce this book and my willingness to pass my skills on to you. Under no circumstances commit a criminal act of theft against me. Due to copyright reasons I do not allow this book to be printed by you.

The CD Rom that is mentioned in this book is given to those studying as a Diploma with me personally. It is not given out for free with this book.

Contents

Disclaimer, Legal Warning and Notice 3
Introduction 5
The Workings of the Mind Model Bulletin Points 9
Seven Important Mind Rules 10
Successful Stop Smoking Session Explained 15
Examples of Real Stop Smoking Clients 16
Start here, Stop Smoking Pre-talk 22
Poisons in Cigarettes 30
Smoker's Mind Model 34
What Do You Know About Hypnosis? 42
Induce Hypnotic Trance 45
Deepening Trance via Staircase 46
Continue by Deepening Trance Further via Bed Image 47
Continue by Deepening Trance Further via Body Parts 47
Continue by Deepening Trance Further if Needed 48
Hypnotic Therapy Session Begins and Ends 49
Pain or Pleasure Suggestion Techniques 49
Pain or Pleasure - Car Crash 50
Pain or Pleasure - Drawing 52
Pain or Pleasure - Russian Roulette 53
Pain or Pleasure - Large Container Image 54
Pain or Pleasure - Death, Pain and Sorrow 55
Pain or Pleasure - Image of One's Self 56
Creative Visualisation of Removing the Past 57

Improve Confidence Relevant to the Session Type, via a Thermometer to 100% Successful 58
Creative Visualisation of Future Image and More..............................59
Associating Good Feeling to an Anchor...61
Post Hypnotic Suggestion..62
End Session by Waking the Client from Trance 64
What to Expect after a Stop Smoking Session 65
Your Journey Continues as this Book Ends...66

Introduction

THOSE STUDENTS THAT HAVE READ MY BOOK: "Beginner to Advanced Practitioner Training Course & Self Development in Psychotherapy Hypnotherapy Neuro-Linguistic Programming (NLP) Cognitive Behavioural Therapy (CBT) Clinical Psychology Vol: 1" will not need to read this book. The information within this book has already been covered in the book just mentioned. Even so, I have also published this script as a separate digital book for those people that requested me to do so.

This book is more than just a stop smoking script. I will also give many examples of real clients that I treated in therapy. I will show you how I structure a set plan for a stop smoking therapy session, and of what needs to be done to help the client overcome their bad habit. Also I will explain to you the knowledge that the client needs to be educated on, in order to help them further. Even though I have a set plan, please remember to always personalise a session to the client within the plan.

The script in this book has been written in a way, not intended to be read out to the clients, word for word. I simply want to show you different beginners and advanced ways of conducting therapy, in a structured session that you can personalise to each client. This script can be adapted and used for other bad habits. I have written both the pre-talk and what is said under hypnosis to the client far longer than it need be. I have done this purposely, to give you more examples of what can be said, so that you can pick and choose what you feel fits that particular client best. So, once again, please note that this script is not intended to be read word for word to the client. It can even be used in a number of sessions, if needed, to make each session different from the previous.

I am David Glenn, a Professional Psychotherapist, Hypnotherapist, NLP Practitioner and Trainer with over twenty year's experience in this profession. I have written this book to pass on my knowledge for those:

1) Interested in the cognitive psychology of oneself as a self-development help guide in understanding and utilising the power of your own mind to overcome: Smoking habit, in order to get the best out of your life by being healthier, free from the negative habit.

2) Wanting to have a successful career in Hypnotherapy, Neuro-Linguistic Programming (NLP), Cognitive Behavioural Therapy (CBT), Life Coaching and Psychotherapy as a whole. Developing or enhancing your therapy skills in dealing with bad habits, to help them recover their cognitive, and physical health, as well as their wellbeing.

Everybody can study this script course book as home study training. It is laid out in layman's terms, so those with no previous knowledge of the subject, can still learn how to use the power of your own mind to enrich your life. Even if you do not want to be a Professional Therapist, you can still study this course to understand yourself more, for self-help and personal development. This will enable you to break negative habits, and have unlimited confidence with the techniques that you can learn and use in your life, or therapy practice to improve your psyche, or that of a client's cognitive health (psychological health) and wellbeing. You will also learn how to hypnotise your clients, friends and family, and find the beneficial power of self-hypnosis.

Enrich your knowledge and skills with what I am going to teach you, which can be used in general life, for yourself and others, or by those wishing a new profession in Hypnotherapy, CBT, NLP Practitioner or Psychotherapist. Keep an open mind to new possibilities. How you have thought, communicated, and acted throughout life, may need to change, or be adapted for positive effect. I will teach you the tools of how this can be done to enable you or others to move on positively in life.

Once you have read and fully understood this book, for many people it is a life changing experience. My philosophy on therapy and psychology in general is - it is the art of understanding the psychology of people, our behaviour, the mind model, body language, communication and speech. You will be able to understand how your mind works, and how to utilise its power for positive change.

Anyone on earth, if able bodied, can drive, or learn to drive a car. Be that as it may, that does not mean you will ever be a professional rally, or formula one racing car driver. In order to be the formula one expert in the psychotherapy world, you have to have that special something: innate quality. You cannot think, act, or communicate as the general public do. In general life, what you think is rude, morally wrong, or what you would not dream of saying to a fellow human being in public, those same rules do not apply in the therapy room, because the client is paying you for a highly skilled service. You must never allow your own personality to effect what needs to be done, in order to help the client progress forwards positively in their lives. Conducting therapy is not about you or your beliefs; it is about what is best for the client, even if you have to be cruel to be kind, and go outside of your comfort zone. You may have thought that therapy is just about counselling, empathy, listening, understanding, relating to, comforting and simply relaxing a person. It is far more complex than that. You are not there to comfort a client; you are there to enable them to become unstuck, get out from their negative mindset, and move forward for positive effect and self-fulfilment. You are there to enable them to see the wood from the trees, so they can find the truth about themselves. Thereby you can support them with education, by imparting psychotherapy knowledge that can be adapted, to enable growth and movement. You will understand this more as you learn, by reading through this book in full.

I have met many students that have all the knowledge they require to be great Hypnotherapist, CBT, NLP Therapists, but yet many lack intuition. This is a skill that you either already have, or you have not. Without it, success as a psychotherapist will be limited. Of course I have also met many students that have no confidence whatsoever, and I watch them grow and develop into great therapists through the knowledge from my training.

I have a very modern approach to therapy for today's generation, as I am sure you will come to realise as we continue. Once you have absorbed all the knowledge I am about to teach you, you will know more than most therapists that have been in the profession for many years. This book contains valuable information on becoming a Professional Hypnotherapist, and Psychotherapist, despite that I still advise all my students to practise on volunteers, for charities, family and friends, before their first paying client. Conducting psychotherapy is an extremely complex and skilful job. Therefore after reading this book, and gaining some practical skills, if you do not feel you have the ability to put in place the knowledge I have imparted in this book, then I will teach you the skills in a group or one on one setting. Through tailor-made training this will enable you to set up in business, with the greatest confidence in knowledge and skills to succeed in a successful psychotherapy career.

Prepare yourself for a truly amazing, life-changing experience. Enjoy as you learn, and I guarantee, at times you will be thinking: WOW! MIND BLOWING, INSPIRATIONAL KNOWLEDGE AND WISDOM, ALL IN THIS BOOK!

My recommendation is to read this book, in its entirety, more than once, to fully understand the connection between each skill being taught. Please do not speed read this book, or skip chapters. Take your time to absorb all the information being taught.

It will also be most beneficial to put the knowledge and skills into practise, by attending my group training workshop sessions or one to one training.

The Workings of the Mind Model Bulletin Points

AS A STUDENT, BEFORE YOU CONDUCT a therapy session with any type of client, you first must learn the mind model and memorise it. I have added the bulletin points of the Mind Model in this chapter to help you.

Three parts of the whole mind:

1) Conscious Mind Functions: Rational logical thought - Makes decisions, but the subconscious determines on whether those decisions are carried out or not - One task at once - Willpower - General speech.

2) Subconscious Mind Functions: Many tasks at once - Memories - Imagination - Emotions - Habits - Protects us - In control - Intelligence - Perception of reality - Habitual speech.

3) Analytical or Critical Area: This part of the mind is the conduit connection between the conscious and subconscious, passing information between the two main parts of the whole mind. It is the part of the mind that reasons to determine new information as being fact or fiction (real or fake), based on information from the subconscious memories.

The subconscious four reference points:

(A) The subconscious mind does not know the difference between what is real or imagined.

(B) The subconscious also does not know the difference between good habits, or bad habits. A habit is a habit through repetition regardless.

(C) The subconscious has no concept of time, past, present or future with regards to associated links.

(D) The subconscious also works via associated links, which are memories, cognitive thought (a persons perception of fact or fiction, real or fake, true or false-truth), and emotions (pain or pleasure), that are associated (connected), within the mind to an anchor. This can be any sound, touch, taste, smell, or seeing a certain person (or behaviour), colour, object or place.

The seven mind rules:

1) Ideas or thoughts result in physical immediate emotional reactions.
2) The subconscious mind delivers what we focus on.
3) Repeated negative or positive focused thoughts result in long-term organic change over time.
4) Imagination overpowers knowledge within in the mind.
5) Fixed thoughts can only be replaced by another via the subconscious.
6) Opposing ideas cannot be held at the same time.
7) Conscious effort alone, results in opposite subconscious success.

Seven Important Mind Rules

MOST PEOPLE WRONGLY BELIEVE that the mind and body are two separate things, but the brain is part of the body as a whole, and the mind is part of the brain. You are one being, so the mind and body are the same whole, because they are connected.

One: Ideas or thoughts result in physical immediate emotional reactions - Thought processes affect the reactions of your immediate behaviour, even if you are not consciously aware of your reaction. For example, a micro-signal in the facial area of looking upset. Negative thoughts of any kind develop instantly into negative, physical, emotional changes within the body. Example: blushing, or imagining being upset, or crying in a certain situation, will result in you doing so, by just the thought of being confronted by that situation. If you imagine a spider is going to hurt you, then the imagined idea causes a physical, emotional, negative reaction to fear, even though the spider is of no danger to you and may not even be there. Thoughts that release powerful emotions, whether real or imagined will, without fail, seep into subconscious mind. Physical, emotional reactions then occur, due to the subconscious accepting the negative thoughts as fact. This is due to the subconscious mind not knowing the difference between what is real or imagined. Of course happy thoughts also have an instant effect on your emotions, and therefore your body as well, by having a positive effect on the body unlike negative thoughts. Consider the mind and body as being the same thing, because the mind is part of the body, therefore whatever thought you have, affects every living cell within your body, either negatively or positively, depending on your thought, so it's best to think positively.

Two: The subconscious mind delivers what we focus on - When wanting to achieve a realistic goal that you are not already doing, if you focus your subconscious mind on a negative, then a negative result is what will be achieved and the goal is failed. Alternatively, by playing a positive movie of achieving that same goal within your imagination, then you will achieve that goal on a conscious level, because your subconscious mind believes you have already achieved it, and that makes it easier to do so via the subconscious auto pilot. The reason the subconscious believes you have already achieved the goal, is because you played the positive movie of doing so, and the subconscious mind does not know the difference between what is real or imagined, because both are your reality. You made a conscious decision to do something, your subconscious then plays a positive movie of what you consciously want to achieve, and by doing so, it makes a task easier to achieve, due to the two parts of the mind working in agreement, instead of being in conflict.

What I have just written above, is in relation to a person that wants to achieve a goal that they should be doing, but are not doing it. However, a person with a bad habit is the opposite, because they are already doing something that they should not be doing, so the focus of the subconscious mind has to be different. A person with a bad habit wrongly focuses the subconscious mind with the association of pleasure to the habit, this positive association must be changed to a negative focused association, in order to stop the bad habit. We are often asked, "Who are you?" The simple answer is to tell the questioner your name. However, that does not really tell them who you are. The real answer is, "I am what I focus my subconscious mind on."

Three: Repeated negative or positive focused thoughts result in long-term organic change over time - When ill, negative, repeated, focused thoughts you have about yourself delay the healing process, and can even kill you with stress due to causing heart failure. When positive with uplifting thoughts, we tend to recover faster from illness. This is the mind and body connection being the same thing. A large percentage of human illnesses are functional as opposed to organic, so continued, negative, focused thoughts that you have about yourself, result in long-term, organic, negative change and therefore illness. The term used is "Psychosomatic" (illness caused by the mind).So, mind rule one and two develops into mind rule three, if the person continues the negative thoughts about them self. People that cause illness through the mind can be classed as neurotic, and the term used for a person that continuously has psychosomatic illness is a hypochondriac. Even though some people have genuine diseases, negative, repeated, focused thoughts will still result in further negative long-term organic change over time. With the use of hypnosis, the effect from the negative, focused thought can be changed, by changing the thought to positive. Be that as it may, a negative thought can also result in positive, organic change. For example: a negative thought towards the bad habit of smoking, means the organic change is better for long-term health due to the client avoiding smoking. Of course positive focused thoughts result in long-term positive health benefits for the mind and body.

Four: Imagination overpowers knowledge within in the mind - A smoker has the conscious knowledge that smoking is killing them, but yet they have not imagined the negative effects within the subconscious mind. The subconscious mind is therefore still playing a positive, imagined, associated movie toward the bad habit, and therefore the person does not change, because imagination has overpowered their knowledge, even though the positive association to the habit is wrong and is killing them. Once again remember that imagination (subconscious mind), is more powerful than knowledge (conscious mind), and the subconscious always wins, even when wrong. In order to do anything in life, you have to first imagine doing it, hence why imagination (subconscious mind), is more powerful than knowledge (conscious mind), within the whole mind. This is why people fail, they have made a conscious decision for change, and then tried to consciously succeed, but it is impossible to consciously stop smoking, or any bad habit, when the subconscious is still playing a positive movie towards the bad habit. Change the positive to a negative within the subconscious and the bad habit is avoided. With regards to people with depression, anxiety, stress, low confidence etc, the movie within their subconscious is of wrongly believing an imagined, negative thought as fact. Example: a person may imagine that it is fact that they are useless, ugly etc, so they feel depressed and fear, even though they are wrong, but the negative, imagined thought is fact in their warped perception of reality. Change the imagined thought to agree with logic knowledge, and the person's reality changes for the positive and the problem is solved.

Five: Fixed thoughts can only be replaced by another via the subconscious - If every morning at 7am I got up and consciously made the decision to tap my head three times with my hand, the subconscious, eventually through repetition, takes the task on as a habit, it has become a fixed thought and it is incorporated into my morning ritual. This habit would then be protected by the subconscious. So to get up one morning and consciously force myself not to tap my head, would result in an overwhelming urge of anxiety, as if something is wrong, as if there is a potential danger. This anxiety of feeling there is a danger, is simply the subconscious mind reminding me to do the habit, because it wrongly feels it is doing me a favour protecting that habit, by keeping me from harm.

In order to overcome this anxiety, and to stop a potential danger, be it real or not, the subconscious reminds me of the habit, so I tap my head for instant relief from anxiety. In other words there is a subconscious resistance to change because the subconscious mind believes it is doing me a favour, so continues to protect the habit even though it is not healthy to do so. Remember the subconscious does not know the difference between a good or bad habit, it protects it regardless, as if there is a danger not to do so. It is simply an associated link between getting up in the morning and tapping my head that became a habit. In other words, repetition that has become a habit through an associated link. Changing the associated link subconsciously, will bring about permanent results.

For example, imagining myself getting up in the morning and doing press-ups, this would occupy my hands so as not to tap my head, and over time the press-ups become a new more positive habit. This is why a smoker always wants a cigarette first thing in the morning, due to the association of waking up and smoking, they have never imagined doing something else and not smoking.

Dear student, as far as the subconscious mind is concerned, what is the difference between the habit of smoking and the habit of me tapping my head? Think about that for a moment.

The answer is no difference, because both habits are protected within the subconscious, both create anxiety if not carried out, they are in fact the same. A habit. So now let me ask, what is the difference between smoking and swimming within the subconscious? The answer is they are the same, because both habits are protected, because the subconscious mind does not know the difference between swimming and smoking, both are a habit regardless of them being good or bad. The habit of swimming is protected to stop you from the danger of drowning if you fall in to a river, and the habit of smoking is protected to save you from potential danger that's not real. Your subconscious doesn't know there is no danger by not smoking, because the smoker has never told the subconscious mind of the danger of doing the habit in the first place. They have associated pleasure to it, so of course they keep smoking. The fixed thought that needs to be changed, needs to be replaced via the subconscious, because that is where the habit is stored, and not in the conscious mind, so of course consciously wanting to change will always result in failure, due to mind rule four: "Imagination overpowers knowledge within in the mind", and a combination of the other mind rules. You are starting to see how these seven mind rules are all connected, and of course they are, because we only have one mind each.

Six: Opposing ideas cannot be held at the same time - This means that once the subconscious has accepted an idea as fact, then any opposing conscious ideas will always be rejected. The subconscious, always conflicts against an opposing idea from the conscious mind, and as you know the subconscious is the stronger part of the mind and therefore, overpowers the opposing conscious idea or thought. That is true unless you change an idea on a subconscious level so that both parts of the mind are in agreement. For example: a person consciously thinks "I want to stop smoking", but they continue to smoke because their subconscious is protecting the habit and positive associated links of smoking, due to them not showing their subconscious any differently. Remember mind rule four: "Imagination overpowers knowledge within in the mind", which means the subconscious overpowers the conscious, and that of course has a detrimental effect on a person's life, and that is why, in order to change, it has to be done subconsciously first, to then be a conscious act. Also the subconscious cannot have two opposing ideas at the same time, for example: it cannot think fact (real) and fiction (not real), towards an idea at the same time, it is one or the other idea. The same with the conscious mind, you cannot logically think something is true and false at the same time. Nonetheless as you now know, the conscious can try to oppose an idea from the subconscious, but again, two opposing ideas cannot be held at the same time, so the stronger more powerful subconscious wins.

Seven: Conscious effort alone, results in opposite subconscious success - Conscious effort alone, results in opposite, subconscious success, means that; if you only consciously attempt to try and achieve your goal, you will fail every time. For example: a stop smoking client consciously thinks, "I don't want that cigarette because I don't need it." They have, by doing so, implanted within the subconscious mind, an image of them wanting it and smoking it, the exact opposite of the conscious thought. So the client then eats the chocolate due to the powerful suggestion of the image in their subconscious mind of doing so. If you say to yourself consciously "Don't think of a black cat", then subconsciously you have thought of one, the opposite of what you wanted to achieve. This is why conscious effort alone will never work to overcome a problem, and as you now know, the subconscious is more powerful than the conscious, and it overpowers the conscious will every time. This is why hypnosis is so successful in helping people overcome any problem.

Successful Stop Smoking Session Explained

A SUCCESSFUL STOP SMOKING SESSION is broken down into three parts:

a) Pre-talk
b) Suggestibility test
c) Hypnosis session

Examples of Real Stop Smoking Clients

Before I explain the pre-talk, I will give you some examples of what my real smoker clients have said in the therapy room. They make up excuses in their own mind in order to take away the guilt of abusing their own body. A person's action of poisoning their own body and their loved ones has harmful effects and they know it is wrong, so they wrongly justify this abuse by their excuses and lies that they tell them self. Most of the time, they are not aware of the lies they tell themselves, until I make the client aware of what they have told me.

For example a client said to me, via habitual speech from a false-truth: "I can stop smoking whenever I like" I then asked: "When was the last time you stopped smoking?" The reply was: "When I got married, I stopped for three months, so I know I can do it." She looked really pleased with herself and I thought this must be an excuse, so I delved deeper by asking: "When did you get married?" She replied: "Ten years ago." So the fact is for ten years this client had been lying to herself that she could stop smoking whenever she liked, as an excuse to abuse her own body, but she was not aware of this until I told her. Remember that the subconscious has no concept of time, so this excuse was new every time it was reinforced as far as her subconscious was concerned. Clients use kidology on themselves to justify buying the poison in the first place, because it first takes away their guilt of buying it, and then second smoking it. Smokers are the same as weight loss clients, in that they will go and join a gym, or buy a bike, or some other form of exercise equipment for the home, and then they only use it twice. Again they have done this to kid themselves into thinking they are doing themselves a favour, because it takes away their guilt when they smoke by telling themselves it's a treat, but since when has self-harm been a treat up to thirty times a day. They then tell themselves: "Haven't I done well, I'm having a treat, a cigarette." Or if stressed they say: "I need a cig." One excuse after another. They will tell you: "I go to the gym," when in fact they have been twice. "I've got a bike," but they never use it etc. I have even had clients take their gym clothes to work with them every day, but after work they just go home. It gives them a moment of pleasure, using kidology on themselves.

Every January a smoking client says or thinks: "Right, new year's resolution for me, I'm going to get fit and stop smoking." That was habitual speech or thought that is a false-truth. They start off with good intentions and then the excuses start. They say to themselves: "Well that party I'm going to a month from now, everyone will be smoking, so I'll stop after that." One excuse after another throughout the year, and before they know it, the whole year has passed and nothing has been done. As a result their health worsens and the excuses have become normal, rational thoughts to them, even though their thought processes are irrational.

I have even had a client say to me: "I can't stop smoking today because my dog has gone missing." "I like the taste of cigarettes," they say, but once I delve deeper it turns out that after the twenty they have smoked each day, they only enjoyed one or two. Yet again another excuse, because it was the cup of tea and sitting down to relax that they enjoyed, but they wrongly associate this pleasure with the cigarette. In fact the cigarette has nothing to do with the pleasure they got from sitting down and relaxing or finishing work. This is a reassociated emotion to the cigarette (anchor) and that must be explained to all clients so that they understand. It is not the cigarette that gives them pleasure, it was the relaxing, which has nothing to do with smoking. If a client thinks smoking relaxes them, then that is their warped perception and lack of understanding of a reassociated emotion and their mind in general. It is simply impossible to relax when smoking because it is a poison, which forces the body to work harder to survive. Even so, the subconscious is so powerful that the self-abuser convinces them self that they have relaxed, when in fact their heart rate has increased to compensate for the poison. Their lungs work harder to take in more oxygen due to the smoke starving their body of oxygen, so again, simply impossible to genuinely relax whilst smoking.

On a Friday they say (habitual speech via a subconscious false-truth): "I'll stop smoking on Monday." This again takes away their guilt of smoking over the weekend. Monday comes and they still smoke, but on the Friday the lie they told themselves made them feel good. Again it wrongly justified their actions of poisoning themselves and their loved ones over the weekend.

"I'm smoking as a treat because I have had a stressful day at work," they say. The fact is they smoke twenty or more times each and every day, so again they need a new excuse. A treat is something we do every blue moon, not twenty times every day and justify it with a lie. We all get stressed but that does not mean we go abuse and ourselves and loved ones with poison.

A client told me that he had not smoked for nine months but then he was knocked off his motor bike and the guy that hit him handed him a cigarette. He then told me: "So from that day I have smoked again." This client was putting the blame of him smoking onto a man that had knocked him off his bike. In a deluded way it took away his responsibility for his own actions and therefore is his warped mind his smoking was not his fault.

"I know I wouldn't be able to just stop because of the craving in my head" one client said. This of course is the client's simple lack of understanding of his mind. The craving will be explained later and how to deal with it.

"I am addicted to nicotine," they say. Well once you have told them the pre-talk (in this book, as shown in the pages to come); they can no longer use addiction as an excuse, because a cigarette is not addictive, as I will later prove.

I ask smoker clients: "Do you drive when smoking?" Most will say: "Yes." I also ask: "Do you smoke when the children are in the car, or another loved one?" The common reply is, "Yes, but I open the window to let the smoke out." I always reply by saying: "That's not why you opened the window at all." I continue by saying: "That is just your conscious perception of the situation. You opened it to take away your guilt of poisoning your own children with those chemicals because you can't tell that smoke to go out of your open car window, in fact you are simply circulating it around the car by opening the window. Therefore even when you are not smoking you are still poisoning your children, due to the fact that you have contaminated the whole car with deadly poisons." I then ask clients: "What is in the dust particles in the seating of your car? The answer is poisons from your cigarettes that your children are breathing in, and being poisoned by. So that cigarette must be more important to you than your own children. It must be, or you would not be poisoning them with it." By saying things of that nature creates a feeling of guilt towards smoking within the client's mind and so I am turning something that was once pleasurable into something that is emotionally painful within the client's subconscious, and that is smoking. You can also say a similar thing when it comes to smoking in their home, poisons in the carpet in the form of dust particles build up from the chemicals from the cigarette they have smoked. So even when the client is not smoking, they are still poisoning their loved ones every time they move around the home, due to them previously contaminating the home. Every time they sit on the settee or walk on the carpet, unseen dust is displaced and goes into everyone's lungs with their chemicals from smoking in it. To eliminate this poison, they need to stop adding to it, by quitting smoking. This may seems a harsh way of stopping people from smoking, still it is reality, and I can assure you it is very successful and very healthy for the client. With regards to smoking in the car, the UK law changed towards the end of 2015 and it is now illegal to smoke whilst driving and if children are in the car then smoking is not allowed at all.

One client told her husband late at night that they had run out of milk and she needed to go and buy some more for breakfast in the morning. She then went to the kitchen and poured all the milk they had down the sink so that she could go to the shop. Of course all this was an act in deluding herself for an excuse just to buy some cigarettes and smoke them. She was hiding, like a child being naughty, due to the husband not knowing she was a smoker.

Many smokers will say that they only smoke when with their mates, as if that justifies it; as if it is their mates fault. They have made an associated link between socialising with mates and smoking. Be that as it may, it is just a social conformity that causes a change of behaviour which is due to social influence. It is social compliance which tells me the smoker is highly suggestible, and that is beneficial, as they make an easy hypnotic subject for change.

Basically not only is it an associated link but they are also smoking when in a group, because they want to be accepted as part of the group. Everyone else is smoking and they do not want to look the odd one out. Make the client aware that society does not see them as the odd one out, by not smoking; other people are looking at their mates in disgust and looking at them as the intelligent one if they are not smoking. This boosts the client's ego and makes them feel better about not smoking when with their mates. Educate the client by saying: "What does a child do when they have been naughty? They make excuses to mummy and daddy saying: "It isn't me, it is someone else's fault." What does a smoker do when they have been naughty smoking? They make excuses just like a child, but instead of making it to mummy and daddy they make it to themselves. So where smoking is concerned you are acting like a child, however that does not mean you are childish, it just means where the cigarette is concerned you are very childlike. Well it's time to start being the adult that you are where cigarettes are concerned."

Dear student, all clients will agree with that once you have pointed out their excuses and lies, and all are grateful to be told. So don't think this is insulting to the clients, because it is not. Simply tell them: "I am telling you this to give you a reality check and by doing so we are saving your life today and the quality of your future happiness, and health in life." The client then feels relieved and relaxes more as a result.

Many clients find smoking an inconvenience, due to trying to find a place to smoke. They even stand outside of their own home, and bars (now that the smoking ban is law in public), in the rain, smoking, freezing to death in the cold just to have a cigarette. They do not realise that they are being controlled by something else, in this case a silly, little white stick. It is like a child having to go outside because they know they are being naughty. Make the client aware of how ridiculous it is as the adult, that they are being controlled by a poison. Make them aware of all the free time that they wasted by smoking. What have they been missing out on? Examples are family time with the children, their favourite TV shows and the extra money etc. I ask the client: "What happens when you run out of cigarettes in the house?" Most will say they never do and that, in itself, shows that their life is so dependent on that silly, little white stick. They start to realise how pathetic that is, so I make the point of asking them: "What do you think about that, do you think it is pathetic?" They all say: "Yes", as more guilt sets in. By saying: "Do you think it is pathetic?" That is an indirect way of calling the client pathetic instead of saying: "You are pathetic," I still suggested it indirectly, which avoided confrontation and has a bigger impact on the client to provoke more guilt in agreement with me, the therapist.

A single mother client told me that if she ran out of cigarettes she would have to go to the shops and buy some more. "What if it is midnight and the kids are in bed?" I asked. "I would have to get them up and put them in the car and take them with me" she replied. The fact is she had done that several times over the years. I then made the point of explaining that her children's sleep is very important to them, for their future development and she agreed. I reinforced the guilt by saying: "That cigarette is once again more important to you than your children's health." The realisation sets in again in the client's mind because she never once considered the many effects smoking has on others. Not only do clients act like children where the cigarette is involved, but they are also extremely selfish people. That does not mean they are selfish in general life, but where the cigarette is concerned they are, due to it being more important than anything else in their life, even their loved ones. All will agree with this because they are starting to understand what they have been doing to their loved ones all these years. Pain and pleasure reversed in the client's mind again. I then asked this same client: "What if you run out of milk or toilet roll, would you do the same and get the kids out of bed to go to the shop?" "Yes," she replied. So I asked: "Have you ever done that?" She said, "No." So the fact is she has run out of essentials in the house but not once has she rushed to the shops the way she had when running out of a cancerous stick, she had instead waited until the morning. Again she starts to realise how selfish, childlike, and pathetic she has been where the cigarette is concerned and all the excuses and lies to herself. The client is rationalising for the first time in her life with regards to the poisonous stick. She told me that when she takes the kids to the shop for cigarettes, late at night, she always buys them sweets. I made her realise that she had not done that as a favour to the kids; she had simply done it out of her own selfishness, to take away her own guilt of getting the kids out of bed to buy a silly white stick. Again she agreed, where as previously she hadn't seen the situation the same as I have.

Once I have made the clients aware of all the excuses that they make in order to wrongly justify their actions of smoking, a large number of them will then unknowingly try to find other excuses. For example: they will ask me if I smoke. They do this because no matter what my answer is, they can throw it back at me as another excuse. If I were to say: "No, I don't smoke," they would then say: "Well, you don't know what it's like, so you can't stop me." If I were to say: "Yes, I smoke," they would then say: "Well if you can't stop smoking you can't stop me." So no matter how I answer with no or yes, I lose, because the client would have taken control of the session by using me as an excuse to continue to smoke. So I make it known to the clients that the only reason they have asked do I smoke is because they want to use me as an excuse, because it makes them feel better about themselves due to the excuse taking away their guilt for a little while. They were trying to use me as an excuse, and therefore in order to prevent the excuse and to prevent them taking control. It is a question I never answer, and nor should you. I would simply say: "It doesn't matter whether I smoke or not because I'm not the one that matters right now, you are, let's move on." Saying: "Let's move on," is a command not a question, so I have kept control of the session, plus I didn't answer the question, so no new excuse was created.

Some clients will tell me that they don't make excuses or blame others, but this is in itself an excuse, because of course they make excuses, if they didn't they wouldn't be poisoning themselves and others. For example: a client that thought she didn't make excuses, I asked her: "Can you afford the two thousand pounds or more a year that you were spending on cigarettes?" She said: "That's the problem, I can." The fact is the problem is not the money, it's the person. She was blaming money and her ability to afford the poisons she was putting in her own body, as if her wealth was the problem. So in short, smokers blame everything and everyone else for their problem, apart from themselves, by making up excuses. It's the partner's fault because he/she wants cigarettes, when in fact they don't. It's the kid's fault, they stress me out. It's work's fault, it's that wedding I've got to go to, I'm addicted etc.

Dear student, what follows is the pre-talk to the hypnotic induction that you can say to the client. I have written both the pre-talk and what is said under hypnosis far longer than need be. I have done this purposely to give you more examples of what can be said; so that you can pick and choose what you may feel fits that particular client best. So, in short, this script is not intended to be read word for word to the client, and please remember that you need to personalise the session. The script can even be used in a number of sessions if needed, to make them different from the previous.

Start here, Stop Smoking Pre-talk

What follows is the Pre-talk to the hypnotic induction. I have written both the pre-talk and what is said under hypnosis, far longer than it needs be. I have done this purposely, to give you more examples of what can be said and so that you can pick and choose what you may feel fits that particular client best. So, in short, this script is not intended to be read word for word to the client. It can even be used in a number of sessions if needed, to make them different from the previous, and please remember to always personalise a session to the client.

I always start by asking the client about their problem and situation to gain the information needed for the session. This time also allows me the time needed to build rapport. I then ask: "Do you agree that there are two parts of the human mind, the conscious mind (their conscious will) and the subconscious mind (their imagination)?" All would tend to agree with that there are two parts.

Dear student, please note, I never mention the third part of the mind, the analytical area of the mind to a client, because they do not need that information. So keep it simple. I only gave that information to you because you are my student, and of course, you are not training a student, they are a client, so the two parts of the mind is all they need to know.

I then ask the client: "Which part of the mind is in control of what you will be doing day-to-day?" And 99% of the time, clients will say: "The conscious mind." This is for two reasons: firstly, most people think they are consciously in control, and secondly, I also lead the client in the direction of saying: "Conscious Mind."

Dear student, how do I lead a client to say: "Conscious mind and why"? Think about that question, because the answer you have already been taught and therefore you know, even if you think you don't know.

This is what I do. I ask: "Do you agree that there are two parts of the mind, the conscious mind and the subconscious mind?" When I say: "Conscious mind," I lift my left hand, and by doing so I have created an anchor within the client's mind of the thought of: "Conscious Mind" being associated to my left hand, which is the anchor. I then put my left hand down and then when saying: "Subconscious Mind," I raise my right hand, and therefore by doing so I have created an anchor (right hand) associated to the words and thought of the: "Subconscious Mind" and then I put my right hand down. I then ask the client: "Which part of the mind is in control of what you will be doing day-to-day?" At the same time of asking that question, I reactivate the anchor with the association of thinking of the: "Conscious Mind" by simply raising my left hand, and so the client is led to answer the question by saying: "Conscious Mind" and then I put my left hand down. I then tell the client: "You are in fact wrong. It is the subconscious mind (reinforce the anchor by raising the right hand) that is in control and I will explain why later in the session" (then drop the right hand). I then reassure them that everyone gets it wrong and that avoids any confrontation and prevents the client from feeling foolish.

Dear student, can you think of why I have done that? Why had I led the client to think and say: "Conscious Mind" when it is wrong? How do I benefit from this as a therapist? Well I benefit in five ways as follows:

First benefit, I now know the client can be led, and therefore they are suggestible, which makes the session easy.

Second benefit, I also created a third anchor, can you work out what the third anchor is? It is not an obvious one, so I wouldn't expect even an experience therapist to figure out what I have done. I'll give you a hint. The first anchor was my left hand associated to thinking of and therefore saying the: "Conscious Mind." The second anchor was my right hand associated to the thought of the: "Subconscious Mind" and the third anchor was created once I said: "You are in fact wrong, it is the subconscious mind." It was at this point that the third anchor was created when I reinforced the second anchor by raising the right hand.

Even though I have given you that information, I still wouldn't expect you to have worked out what the third anchor is or what it is for, if you have, then well done you. When I lifted my right hand a second time I was reinforcing the second anchor to the thought of the subconscious mind. However because at that point I had made the client aware that the subconscious was the right answer, I had also then quickly changed the second anchor (right hand) to now thinking it's right (correct answer). So now the second anchor's association has been changed from thinking of the subconscious mind to realising it is right, it is the correct answer. Once the new association to the anchor (right hand) was created, I put my right hand down, so that the associated link to being right remained to be used again later in the session.

So I can class this as a new second anchor or third anchor with the original association to the second anchor having now been replaced. Remember the subconscious can only ever remember the last thing that was associated to an anchor. In this case the new thought of knowing it is right (correct answer) to the anchor of the right hand. The original association to the second anchor was: "Subconscious Mind" but that association had served its purpose and was no longer needed, so I replaced it for the added benefit of leading the client to associate the right hand to represent the right answer, the correct answer, which implies the right thing to do. I can use this anchor later in the session when I want to provoke, or lead the client to the right answer to whatever future question I ask them. Notice that I use the right hand for the right answer and not the left, hence why: "Conscious Mind" association was left hand, as it was the wrong answer. If I had made the right hand as the anchor for the wrong answer, then it would not have had the same use, and it would have been confusing for the client due to the word: "Right" hand being used for wrong and not right. Always use right hand anchor for a leading signal for the right answer or right thing to do, as in my opinion it should be. I will be using this signal anchor later in the script.

Third benefit of leading the client to say: "Conscious Mind" is the creation of a "Trans-Derivational Search (TDS)" within their mind by me replying with saying: "You are in fact wrong, it is the subconscious mind that is in control and I will explain why later in the session." By saying that I created a: "Trans-Derivational Search (TDS)" within the client's mind because they are now consciously wondering how could they be wrong. How can it be the subconscious that is in control, and I wonder how he is going to explain this? This sent the conscious mind on a journey and therefore bypassed via TDS, which opens up their subconscious to suggestion, which cements the anchor of right hand meaning right answer, the right thing to do.

Fourth benefit is that the client's subconscious knows I am in control. When a client is led to answer wrongly, they accept that they were wrong because I proved to them, with my knowledge that I am right. The client knows that I am right, and so they will agree to all future suggestions and commands from me as being right. I have become the authority figure of reason, truth and knowing what is right. My knowledge gains the clients trust in me. This way I avoid confrontation within the session because the client knows I must be right throughout, regardless of any opposing ideas they may have previously had.

Fifth benefit is that the client is now in light trance due to the TDS and rapport built.

I continue by asking for information about the client, that way I can personalise the session to suit them. I need to know what have they tried in the past, and what their routine is at the moment, and then I have a choice of if I use the answers or not within in the session. As I ask questions I am taking the opportunity to build rapport with the client. I personalise the pre-talk based on the information the client provides. I ask other questions to what I have already asked, for example:

1) How many cigarettes do you smoke a day?
2) When did you start smoking? (The answer to this question gives me the age of the associated smoking links).
3) What methods have you tried to stop smoking?
4) Have you had any success with any of those?

5) Why do you want to stop smoking now? (I am finding an anchor that may be used for positive or negative association depending on the answer).
6) What's the most important reason for you stopping?
7) Name family members, do they smoke? And do you love them?
8) Tell me about a happy time in your life, but if you can't think of one straightaway then imagine a time when you would feel like that.
9) What are your ambitions in life? Etc.....

The information gathered from the above questions can be used later in the session. The more information I have on their problem, the more successful the session will be. For instance, if their reason to stop smoking was for their children's sake or their own health, I would ask for more information on this and therefore the session becomes more personal to them. I continue the pre-talk by telling my clients: "The information you give me I can use to help you later in the session. Personalised sessions are far more successful than a group session. That is why I do not do group sessions, because each individual is different and you are the only person that matters at the moment."

Dear student, saying that, makes the client feel important and of course they are. If the client says: "I enjoy smoking." You would say to the client: "How many of those thirty that you smoke everyday do you enjoy?" Client replies: "Probably three or four." You: "Well it takes about four minutes to smoke a cigarette, so that's 4 x 4 equals 16 minutes of your idea of enjoyment. Now of course it is affecting your health, but what is your health when you get sixteen minutes of enjoyment? And you don't mind those coughs and colds you get, or when you have that coughing in the mornings, and you said it makes you smell, but what is personal hygiene when you have those sixteen minutes. You do not mind standing out in the rain and cold to have that cigarette, and wasting thousands of pounds on smoking, when you have told me you can't afford to go on holiday. It will probably take five to ten years off your life, but just between you and me, what is living as long as you can, when you have those sixteen minutes of deluded enjoyment. Is it worth it? Of course it's not."

"Do you think you are addicted to nicotine?" I ask, because it is a very common belief to most smokers that they are addicted when in fact they are not, so most client will reply: "Yes." "So if you were not addicted to nicotine it would be easy for you to stop, right?" "Yes" is the common reply. "So would it surprise you if I told you that nicotine is not addictive? Because the fact is that nicotine it is not addictive. About five years ago the American government got the top chemists and scientists in America to do a study into nicotine. A million dollars and a six hundred page report later, they found nicotine was not addictive. Now, if you compare nicotine to something that is addictive, like heroin, then someone trying to give up heroin will get shakes, sweats, heart palpitations, sickness, nausea, even hallucinations. Compare that to someone trying to give up cigarettes, they might get a bit bad tempered, but they do not get any real physical symptoms. Also, a heroin addict cannot sleep through the night without their body waking them up for more use of heroin, as soon as the heroin wears off; they have to put more of the heroin into their system just to keep them going. The only heroin addict that can sleep through the night is also an alcoholic, because the alcohol numbs the senses, so they can get a good night's sleep, but when they wake up in the morning they have got to have all the heroin that they have missed from the night, just to get out of bed.

Now when was the last time you woke up in the early morning for all the cigarettes you did not smoke during the night? You do not need all the cigarettes that you missed from the night before just to get yourself out of bed in the morning. Yes, you might think you need one or two, but not all the ones you missed from the night before. You may have gotten out of bed due to not being able to sleep or to go to the toilet, and then had a cigarette. But the cigarette was not the reason you got up, it was just an afterthought. In contrast, a drug addict gets up specifically for more drugs.

So that is twenty or so cigarettes during the day, but none at night and that is because nicotine is not addictive.

What about the nicotine replacement therapies such as patches and gum? Did you know that one day's supply of patches is equivalent to 120 cigarettes? So, that is the equivalent to six packets of cigarettes. Every patch you put on your arm, you are getting ten times more nicotine into your system than you are ever going to get from smoking, so they don't work as advertised to help to stop smoking. The patches work on a placebo effect, if you read the back of the packet and believe what it says and you put that patch on your arm and believe it will help you, you stand a chance of stopping. Of course you still have to go through all the cravings and withdrawals because hypnosis has not been used. Our government did a study a couple of years ago and they found that in people trying to give up smoking by using nicotine gum, only 10% would be successful, and people using patches, 16% of those people would be successful. Now there is not a great deal of difference between any of those figures, but if you turn those figures around the right way, that means 84 to 90% of people using patches, or gum, failed, which means it does not work. What they are trying to tell you is that nicotine is a terrible, addictive chemical and that the patch or the gum is going to replace the nicotine that you used to get from the cigarette. Well here is the thing; a heroin addict tries to break the addiction by taking a substitute drug called methadone, which blocks the craving for the heroin. Now these so-called experts are trying to tell you that nicotine is addictive and of course there is nicotine in cigarettes, but the way that they are claiming to get you from smoking cigarettes is to give you a patch that has more nicotine in it than any cigarette you have ever smoked in your life. So it is just a different way of getting nicotine into your body, and not a way of eliminating nicotine from your body. Why doesn't that increase the addiction to nicotine? It is because nicotine is not addictive. I mean it is like giving a heroin addict more of the heroin to come off heroin, it would not work. And why, if nicotine is meant to be addictive, don't you get hooked on the patches? The answer is again simply because nicotine is not a substance addiction. Why aren't there clinics up and down the country weaning people off patches? There are clinics up and down the country getting people off heroin, but there is not one clinic set up to get people off patches. Why? Because nicotine is not addictive and that is why no one has ever come to me and said: "Please help me come off these nicotine patches. Who makes nicotine patches and gum? The sister company of the company that is losing money on falling sales of cigarettes. So they thought, let's tell these mugs they are addicted to nicotine and when they have had enough, we can make more money from telling them that they now need these nicotine patches to come off the nicotine. Cigarettes advertising is the world's best marketing campaign and they have made a mug of all smokers."

Dear student, notice that I have indirectly called the client a mug. I do that because I want them to feel stupid for having smoked in the past, in order create guilt within their mind. No one wants to be a mug and feel conned, so more neurological pain is associated to the thought of smoking (anchor) and therefore smoking is avoided.

Continue by saying: "So, why did (did meaning past tense) you smoke? It was (was meaning past tense) a habit? Now it might seem a little trivial to say it was (was meaning past tense) just a habit, but smoking is probably one of the most powerful habits there is, due to the psychological addiction and not the substance addiction. You psychologically thought smoking relaxed you but that is impossible, due to the poisons in the cigarette. Smokers think they smoke to relax, but you cannot smoke and relax because Nicotine is a poison and every time you smoked, it made your heart increase by ten beats a minute, as your body tries to cope and get rid of the nicotine poison. But that was a losing battle when you kept adding more poison into your body. Also you've got the carcinogens and phenotrins in cigarettes; they are the cancer producing agents. Now, if you add a drink of tea or coffee to that, and of course there is caffeine in tea and coffee, then you've got four strong stimulants literally making your body race, so you cannot smoke and relax, it is impossible and even less so with the added caffeine drink. Your body was taking in more oxygen to try and compensate for the poisons, so your breathing increased, so again impossible to relax. However your subconscious is so powerful that you convinced yourself that you were relaxing, when in fact your body was not, due to having to work harder to combat the poisons. You only relaxed within your mind and not physically, regardless of whether you thought you had.

You also psychologically thought you enjoyed the cigarette, when in fact it was the socialising or finishing work that you enjoyed, and that good feeling emotion, you wrongly reassociated to the anchor of a cigarette, hence why smoking was a psychological addiction and not substance addiction. You woke up in the morning and you had that first cigarette, and by doing so you were reinforcing the bad habit, then twenty times a day throughout the day you smoked and reinforced the habit over and over again. So it was a conditioned habit and the only reason you did it for so long, was because you were still reinforcing the habit, which was a psychological addiction. People wrongly think they can stop smoking by cutting the number down of cigarettes they smoke each day, but that doesn't work, because the habit is still being reinforced, so in order to stop you need to stop all together today. Which is where I am helping you today. Because it was just a habit, means you can stop and in fact have stopped here today, but you must give up all your psychological addiction excuses.

Dear student, repeat the excuses the client has told you i.e.: I can't stop because it's Monday etc, in order to make them realise how ridiculous the excuses are, so that they can be eliminated as excuses to smoke. However if none are given at this point of the session then wait till later in the session when the client has more understanding of the mind model and therefore them self. Also later, they may be more relaxed if not already, to free up the subconscious excuses that they had previously not been aware of. Help the client understand excuses by sharing with them other client's excuses from your experience that they may relate to, with that being said you can use the excuses I have shared with you until your own experiences build.

I ask my clients: "Did you smoke at times of stress?" "Yes, if it wasn't for the stress of my job or life in general I'd be able to give up easily." This is the common answer that my clients give me. I say: "When do you work?" Client says: "Monday to Friday." I say: "How many did you smoke over the weekend?" Client says: "Thirty a day." I say: "How many did you smoke during the week?" Client says: "Thirty a day." I say: "You have been smoking the same amount, day in day out regardless of if you had a good day or not? You would be lying on the beach in the middle of the summer stress free and still smoking thirty a day. Stress is a silly, childlike excuse, but that is all it is, so it's time to be an adult where your past smoking habit is concerned. Then you have the old faithful excuse: "I don't have any willpower." Now I know you have got willpower, because if you didn't then you would not get out of bed in the morning, or do the hundreds of things you have to do every day that you do not want to do. So you do use your willpower and you do what you don't want to do but had too. So you have got willpower, you have just got to use it to stop smoking as you have today, because you have had the willpower to come for help. Once you have put all these excuses to one side, and there will be more, you are left with just the habit. You know that nicotine is not a substance addictive drug and all the excuses are just that, excuses. So let us look at what we are going to do about this habit. But first I want to tell you about the poisons in cigarettes."

Poisons in Cigarettes

Tar - is a term that describes a collection of solid particles that smokers inhale when they light a cigarette. It is a mixture of lots of chemicals, many of which can cause cancer. When it settles, tar forms a sticky, brown residue that can stain smokers' teeth, fingers, lungs, blood vessels and causes strokes. Because tar is listed on packs, it is easy to believe that it is the only harmful part of cigarettes. But some of the most dangerous chemicals in tobacco smoke are present as gases, and do not count as part of the tar. This means that cigarettes with less tar still contain all the other toxic chemicals, and some of them are listed below.

Arsenic - is one of the most dangerous chemicals in cigarettes. It causes cancer, as well as damages the heart and its blood vessels. Small amounts of arsenic can accumulate in smokers' bodies and build up to higher concentrations over months and years. As well as any direct effects, it can worsen the effect of other chemicals by interfering with our ability to repair our DNA and as a result smokers physically age faster than they would have if they had not smoked.

Benzene - is a solvent used to manufacture other chemicals, including petrol. It is well established that benzene can cause cancer, particularly leukaemia. It could account for between a tenth and half of the deaths from leukaemia caused by smoking. Tobacco smoke contains large amounts of benzene and accounts for a big proportion of our exposure to this poison. The average smoker inhales about ten times more benzene than the average non-smoker. And some studies have estimated that the amount of benzene that a person inhales through second-hand smoke over their lifetime can increase their risk of cancer.

Cadmium - is a metal used mostly to make rechargeable batteries. The majority of cadmium in our bodies comes from exposure to tobacco smoke. Smokers can have twice the amount of cadmium in their blood as non-smokers.

Studies have found that the amounts of cadmium present in tobacco smoke are capable of affecting our health, its dust and fumes are toxic. It is a known cause of cancer, and can also damage the kidneys and the linings of the arteries. Our bodies have proteins that absorb harmful chemicals like cadmium, but the amounts in smoke can overload these proteins. Cadmium can also prevent our cells from repairing damaged DNA. Because of this, it can make the effects of other chemicals even worse.

Formaldehyde - is a smelly chemical used to kill bacteria, preserve dead bodies and helps to manufacture other chemicals. Did you ever stop to think why a cigarette never rots? It is one of the substances in tobacco smoke most likely to cause diseases in our lungs and airways. Formaldehyde is also a known cause of cancer. Small amounts in second-hand smoke could increase our lifetime risk of cancer. Tobacco smoke is one of our major sources of formaldehyde exposure. Places where people smoke have three times the normal levels of this poison.

Polonium - is a radioactive element and polonium-210 is its most common form. Polonium strongly emits a very damaging type of radiation called Alpha Radiation that can usually be blocked by thin layers of skin. But tobacco smoke contains trances of polonium, which become deposited inside your airways and deliver radiation directly to surrounding cells. The lungs of smokers can be exposed to four times more polonium than those of non-smokers and specific parts may get a hundred times more radiation. One study estimated that someone smoking one and half packs a day receives the equivalent amount of radiation as someone having 300 chests X-rays a year.

Chromium - is a metal used to make metallic alloys, dyes and paints and comes in different types; "Chromium III" or "Trivalent chromium" is most commonly used. It is available as dietary supplements and is harmless. On the other hand, "Chromium VI" and "Hexavalent Chromium" are very toxic, and they are found in tobacco smoke, and are known to cause lung cancer. Chromium allows other cancer causing chemicals (such as polycyclic aromatic hydrocarbons) to stick more strongly to DNA and damage it, which causes premature ageing, cancer and overall ill health.

1, 3-Butadiene or BDE - is an industrial chemical used in rubber and resin manufacture. Some scientists believe that of all the chemicals in tobacco smoke, BDE may present the greatest overall cancer risk and it is found in large amounts in tobacco smoke.

Polycyclic Aromatic Hydrocarbons or PAHs - are a group of powerful cancer causing chemicals that can damage DNA and set cells down the road to becoming tumours. One of these chemicals, Benzo (a) Pyrene or BAP is one of the most widely studied of all tobacco poisons. BAP directly damages p53, a gene that normally protects our bodies against cancer.

Nitrosamines - are a group of chemicals that can directly damage DNA, like Polycyclic Aromatic Hydrocarbons (PAHs). They are found in small amounts in food, but tobacco products, including those that are chewed rather than smoked, are by far our largest source of exposure to these chemicals. Even though they are found in relatively small amounts in cigarettes, they are very strong cancer causing chemicals.

Acrolein - is a gas with an intensely irritating smell and is one of the most abundant chemicals in cigarette smoke. It belongs to the same group of chemicals as formaldehyde and acetaldehyde, both of which can cause cancer.

Until now, it wasn't clear if Acrolein causes cancer as well, but recent experiments suggest that it can. We now know that Acrolein can cause DNA damage that is similar to the damage seen in lung cancer patients. Since smoke contains up to 1,000 times more Acrolein than other DNA damaging chemicals, it could be a major cause of lung cancer. Acrolein also stops our cells from repairing DNA damage, the same as arsenic and cadmium. And the same as hydrogen cyanide, it kills the hairs that normally clean our lungs of other toxins.

Some of the other cancer causing ingredients in tobacco smoke also include metals such as: nickel, lead, cobalt and beryllium. While you may be exposed to some of these metals through domestic items or food, inhaling them in tobacco smoke is worse, because they are easily absorbed by the lungs. Acetaldehyde is also formed in your tissues when you drink alcohol. It is responsible for many nasty hangover symptoms. Also Hydrazine, a very toxic chemical used mainly in rocket fuel.

Continue by saying to the client: "Considering you are breathing in these chemicals twenty or more times a day with each and every cigarette you smoked. Why are you not already dead? (Pause) because there are small trances of those chemicals in each and every cigarette, therefore instead of killing you instantly, you are killing yourself over a period of years as your health deteriorates, which is affectively destroying your quality of life, lessening your life by up to fifteen years and giving you a long, slow and painful death.

Let us say that you grow your own tobacco plant and make your own cigarette from that plant once you have dried the leaves out. Now let us light this cigarette with a flame and take the flame away. What happens? (Pause) Will the cigarette you have made yourself burn? Does a dry leaf burn once the fuel source is taken away, which was the flame from the lighter? Of course not, but yet the cigarette you have bought from the shop does, no matter which way you hold the cigarette it burns. Is it natural for a flame to burn downwards? No. So what is making the cigarette that you have bought from the shop burn, regardless of which way you hold it? (Pause) that's right, all the chemicals in it and that is why the one you have made yourself won't burn, because it has no chemicals in it.

Let us now put the cigarette you have made yourself in a dry place and come back to it in a week's time. What has happened to it? (Pause) That's right, it has rotted because a bacterium has gotten to it. Does a dry leaf stay there forever? Of course not, so the cigarette you have made yourself rots. Why is that? Well because it has no preserving chemicals in it. Formaldehyde being one of them, that we put in dead people to preserve them. The cigarette you buy from a shop, let us put that to one side in a dry safe place and come back to it ten years from now. What has happened to it? (Pause) nothing it is the same cigarette and you can still smoke it, preserved with chemicals that you and your loved ones have been breathing in when smoking and from the contamination on your clothes etc. So those chemicals are for added taste, to preserve the cigarette to keep its shape and to help it burn. Those same chemicals are what have been killing you and your loved ones slowly."

Smoker's Mind Model

The following is said to the client. "The mind is split up into two parts; you have got the conscious and the subconscious parts of the mind. At the beginning of this session you thought that you were consciously in control of your life, however as we continue you will realise that the conscious is the part of the mind that we would like to think is in control, but it is not, it is the subconscious mind that is in control.

For example: you do not think about breathing, blood circulation, making your heart beat, because the subconscious is the auto pilot for the body, it is running the body twenty four hours a day, seven days a week. This part of the mind can do many things at a time and whilst it is running the body, it is also taking in two million pieces of information every second, passing on what it thinks is important to the conscious mind and disregarding the rest. For example: you buy a new car and you are driving down the road in your new car, and now it seems like every other car is the same as yours, they are even the same colour. Even though you cannot remember seeing so many of these same cars the day before, so did everyone go and buy the identical type of new car at the same time as you? No, of course not, it is just the day before the subconscious noticed all these cars, but it thought that type of car was not important to you, so did not pass the information on to the conscious mind. Therefore you were not fully aware of them even though they were there and you saw them. But now you have this new car, it has got to be important to you because you first imagined buying and driving the car and then you consciously did what you had previously imagined. Because in order to do anything in life, we have first got to imagine doing it, so because you imagined it and then did it, the subconscious realises this car is now important to you and so now it passes the information on every time it sees this type of car, so you are now consciously aware of seeing more of those cars than you have ever seen in your life. You see the two parts of the mind have become friends where the thought of this car is concerned.

That is what you have not done with your smoking (or any other bad habit) you have never imagined yourself not smoking so there is still conflict with the conscious and subconscious mind and when the will (conscious) and imagination (subconscious) are in conflict, the imagination always wins, due to the subconscious being the more powerful part of the whole mind. You see you have made a conscious decision to stop smoking but you have not been able to, because you tried to solve your problem on a conscious level, but your problem is within your subconscious mind, let me explain. The conscious part of the mind is very logical and very rational; it is the part that you use when making your decisions on a day-to-day basis, but it is the imagination (subconscious) that determines on whether we carry out those conscious decisions or not. Last week you may have made the conscious decision to go swimming, but then you imagined that the water was cold. How do you know? You did not go swimming because this imagined negative thought of the water being cold stopped you doing something in which you had made a conscious decision to do. Therefore your subconscious mind is in control. This is what has happened with your bad habit problem. You consciously want to stop the bad habit. But you are playing a different movie within your subconscious imagination, again conflict is at work, so you will never stop smoking when only trying consciously. The conscious mind is the part where your willpower is held, but of course, you have got to remember to use it. I know you can use it because you had the will to get up this morning, wash and clothe yourself, so we know it is there.

The conscious part of your mind can think of only one thought or idea at once, this is why we can only concentrate on doing one task at a time when doing it consciously, although, we can still do many tasks at once, but only one is conscious and the others are subconscious in the form of a habit, be it a good or bad habit. The conscious mind is a very a slow part of the mind, and this is why we get stressed out, we try to do too many things at the same time consciously and our minds cannot do it. You know what happens, the phone rings, the children want your attention and you are trying to cook the evening meal, you are stressed out because you are trying to do all three tasks at once. Take a step back, realise what is happening and do one task at a time. Doing one task does not get us stressed; trying to do two tasks consciously starts the stress ball rolling. It is like a snowball rolling down a hill, the more tasks you try to do at once the more the stress builds up, and once we get stressed out, we are then not able to do any of the tasks we were trying to do. Stop, take a step back in your mind, realise what is happening and why you are stressed and do just one task at a time to remove or limit the stress. Due to the stress build up described, you then needed comforting, due to the negative emotion, and you started smoking. The first time this happened, you consciously put the cigarette to your lips and had a drag. You probably felt guilty, but you kept going as a deluded comfort, which can be for emotional or conditioned reasons. Then over time, several cigarettes later, the subconscious part of the mind said: I can do that job for you and it took it on as a habit to free up your conscious mind's burden, so your subconscious thinks it is doing you a favour. Because all a habit is, is something you do consciously a number of times and then the subconscious will take it on as a habit. The subconscious part of the mind knows that you can only consciously concentrate on doing one task at a time, so the more jobs the subconscious can do on your behalf the better. So as far as the subconscious is concerned, it is doing you a favour by taking on the problem as a habit because also the subconscious does not know it is a problem, it is just a habit that you want to do as far as your subconscious is concerned and it will keep the habit until you subconsciously remove the habit by changing the positive associated link to a negative one, so that you avoid the bad habit, and we will do that via hypnosis later. Driving is another habit, again when you first started to learn to drive you drove consciously, you had to think about mirror, signal, brakes, clutch and what is going on around you, it was cognitively exhausting due to being conscious thought. It was impossible to have a conversation or think about what you did the day before or what to do later in the day, again due to the conscious mind only being able to do one task at once and that was driving. But later, over time, you passed your test and practised and so now you do not even need to think about how to drive. You are driving down the road and someone pulls out in front of you and you just stop, you did not have to consciously think about stopping, it happened subconsciously. When you drive home from work, before you know it, you are home and cannot consciously remember the details of most of the journey you have just had, even though you know the journey you have taken because you take the same route every day, so your subconscious has taken it on as a habit, so you subconsciously drove home. That is called: "Highway Hypnosis" because you are no longer consciously driving and that is why you can now have a conversation when driving and you can think of other thoughts. Your life is full of habits. Swimming is a habit, riding a bike, reading, walking, the way you brush your teeth in the morning, because you no longer need to give it any conscious thought, they are all now subconscious actions.

Our lives are full of habits because all habits are created by something you first did consciously a number of times that is then taken on by the subconscious as a habit. Now at the moment the subconscious is protecting these habits, it does not want you to forget to drive as you drive down the road, it does not want you forget how to swim whilst swimming across a river. It is also protecting the habit of overeating (or whatever the bad habit is) because the subconscious does not know the difference between a good or bad habit; a habit is a habit as far as the subconscious is concerned, so it is still playing the old memory for why you wanted to smoke in the first place. It is still running the memory of something that your subconscious still thinks you want to do, so you are fighting between the two parts of your mind. The conscious knows all the reasons why you want to stop smoking or drinking), but the subconscious is still rerunning the old reasons for why you started smoking in the first place. That is why when you try and give up by using willpower alone, the conscious mind gets the cravings, because you say to yourself, right, I'm not going to smoke.

Now the evening comes along and the subconscious knows you always had cigarettes in the evening, so when you do not have a smoke it sets off an alarm in your head to remind you, which makes you feel anxious until you once again carry out the bad habit. If you still do not have that cigarette in your mouth it starts to produce cravings and desires, because the subconscious is reminding you to do something that it thinks you still want to do, it is reminding you of the habit. You have seen this craving as a negative thing and given into it, in a delusional attempt to feel better. But this craving is a positive thing because it means you have won by not smoking in that moment. This is where the habit of smoking then becomes an associated link, let me explain.

The subconscious holds all your memories, you have got memories stored within your subconscious going all the way back to childhood, but you cannot consciously always recall them, but then a song might come on the radio and all of a sudden you can remember a memory that you have associated to that song, who you were with, what you were doing, even what you were wearing in that past time and the emotions you felt. You see the human mind works by association, when we experience two things together for a little while, one will automatically remind us of the other in the future. So, for example: when you are in a situation that is depressing, boring, or stressful, you turn to cigarettes as a deluded comfort. You have created a habit, then you have associated stress to certain situations signalling to your subconscious mind to make you smoke through emotional, habit conditioned reasons, as if the subconscious is doing you a favour to comfort you, when in fact the habit is destroying your health and quality of life. Also in the subconscious are all your emotions, for example: you do not think, I have been in a good mood for the last seven days; I am going to make a conscious decision to wake up in a bad mood tomorrow. All your emotions are controlled by the subconscious. So, due to the habit, you smoke subconsciously once that negative emotional association has been triggered via there activated anchor of stress, depression whatever the anchor may be. By doing so this gives you a delusional sense of pleasure, but then later guilt sets in and you are back where you started, feeling stressed and smoking again, which stresses and damages your body even more. Over time you have created many associated links towards smoking. For example: getting in the car and lighting up. Because this habit formed associated link is in the subconscious mind, you subconsciously smoke without knowing how many cigarettes you have had. To consciously attempt to give into this powerful associated link, that your mind's subconscious created through a habit, would be impossible. You have got to do it on a subconscious level through the imagination, because that is where the problem is. It is the associated link that we need to change later in the session by making a new negative associated link to replace the old positive one of smoking, and also we need to change the association to a positive one of not smoking. Also where you once associated doing the bad habit, we need to change the association to the anchor of doing something else in that same place instead of self-abuse.

The reason you have not been able to stop smoking is because your imagination is in the subconscious and the imagination is very powerful. For example: you have probably had dreams or nightmares before and you have woken up shaking, sweating and your heart pounding, but yet you have not been anywhere, you are still in bed. Well this is because the subconscious part of the mind does not know the difference between something real or imagined, both are your reality. So if you are having this dream of running down the road scared, as far as the subconscious is concerned it is actually happening, therefore it makes physical changes to the body, hence you wake up shaking, sweating and your heart pounding. So that is what you do in a session with me, you use the imagination under hypnosis, because if you imagine that it is going to be easy to stop smoking, then you are right, but if you imagine it is going to be difficult you are also right. You see if you imagine it is going to be easy to stop smoking, then your subconscious will make it easy for you.

The problem is that in the past a lot of the time when you tried to stop smoking, you are consciously saying to yourself: "I will not smoke that cigarette". Well, what are you imagining when you say that? Yes that is right, you are imagining smoking. So you are getting the subconscious to imagine you smoking what you know is wrong for you, and that is making it difficult for you to stop because you have implanted a powerful suggestion of smoking, you then smoke. This is because when the will (conscious) and imagination (subconscious) are in conflict, the imagination will always win because it is the more powerful part of the mind. For example: if you consciously think, do not think of a black cat, you have then imagined a black cat, making it impossible to stop imagining the cat. What you consciously wanted to achieve: "Do not think of a black cat" has had the opposite effect on the subconscious mind and this thought is acted upon just the same as consciously thinking I don't want that cake. You have gone about your bad habit problem consciously and it has had the opposite effect, don't think of smoking consciously, so you subconscious imagines smoking, and therefore you do so.

Now what you have got to do is imagine it is going to be easy for you to stop smoking, you need to imagine not smoking instead of imagining smoking. You have, as I have mentioned, got associations with certain activities and smoking, for example: first thing in the morning or whilst driving, and certain times when you regularly smoke. Now imagine those situations without the cigarettes, which is what you need to do, for example: if you smoke in the evening, you can imagine that morning that you are going to have an evening without the cigarettes and eating fruit instead.

Because you have imagined doing that, without having cigarettes, when the evening comes your subconscious just makes it easy for you not to smoke. Because you have already imagined what is going to happen, that you were not smoking at that time, so the habit formed associated link is broken and the subconscious remembers the new healthier habit link of eating fruit for example. You see you have been telling yourself on a conscious level that you want to stop smoking, but you have not been able to because your smoking problem is within the subconscious mind, even though you are consciously aware of it, you have never told the subconscious it is time to change, the emotional, subconscious and conditioned smoking problem. You have been going about your smoking problem all wrong, and that is where I come in, to help you on a subconscious level through hypnosis.

So this is where hypnosis comes in, there is no magic trick or waving of a magic wand with hypnosis, it is a way of getting you to relax, and because you are relaxed I can talk directly to your subconscious, the part that is in control. Because I am talking to the subconscious, together we can rerecord an up-to-date memory that smoking etc, is bad for you and it is something you do not want to do. So we are taking away the old memory and replacing it with the new memory of not wanting to smoke. Now there is no need for cravings and desires because you have both parts of the mind working as one to keep you away from cigarettes forever. Be that as it may, if a craving does happen then enjoy it, because it means you have won, you are not doing the habit and therefore within a short time the craving stops. As mentioned, the primary function of the subconscious is to protect habits and by doing so it thinks it is protecting you; we know this because if pulled under the water when swimming, you automatically go to the surface and subconsciously swim, due to the protected habit of swimming. The subconscious is there to protect you, so with my help, using hypnosis, it will know that the habit associated conditioned links of smoking is bad for you, and is no longer needed. It will keep you free from the poison in the future. So with hypnosis we are going to replace the old habit with a new memory of not wanting to smoke, and take the habit of smoking away. We are going to get you to use your imagination to imagine so that it is easy to stop, then it will be. By doing so we are going to remind the subconscious that it has got to protect these new healthy associated links and habits. You now see how easy to kick the habit, it is a simple state of mind."

Dear student, basically explain the mind model to the client and cover the four reference points of the mind, and the seven mind rules were appropriate to their problem. There is one more thing to add to your script, with regards to the mind model. That is, the subconscious mind has no concept of time, so it will be easy to overcome the client's problem. You could say to your client:

"You see the human mind works by association. When we experience two things together for a little while, one (the anchor), will automatically remind us of the other (associated memory and emotions), in the future. That is also proof that the subconscious mind has no concept of time. Remember the subconscious mind reference point (C): "The subconscious mind has no concept of time, past, present or future." The associated links of memory and emotions to the anchor, will be the same age twenty years from now, the same age from the day you created the anchor, so you will still remember the event and (or just), feel those same emotions that you have associated to the song, as if you were back in that time, the day you created the anchor. This is due to the subconscious mind not realising that twenty years have gone by, it is as if it were yesterday. Your physical body has aged, but those associated links to the anchor, are the same age as the day they were created, and therefore the subconscious mind has no concept of time. This means that memories and emotions within the subconscious do not age, and also a memory and emotion are two separate things from the same event, hence why a memory can be repressed and the emotion be remembered. Why the memory can be repressed was explained in my Beginners to Advanced Volume One Book. Of course you consciously know past, present and future, but that is not where the associated links to the anchor are stored. A memory, emotion (associated links to an anchor), are stored within the subconscious. Even though a memory and emotion cannot be changed and are the same age throughout life, we can still create a new memory and emotion of the same event to the same anchor, in order to replace the old, via the subconscious, using hypnosis. This way we rationalise an event through an adult's perspective, instead of the child's old perspective, so that any negative effect that the associations to an anchor were causing, can be removed and replaced for new positive associations."

Dear student. In this script I am simply showing another way of explaining the information to make it more personal to the client's problem. Reading this script of ideas, you will realise that what the client is told, and what I have taught you to do as a therapist, the skills, the understanding of the client's problem and the way they think, and how I advise of how you need to think, are two very different mindsets. The therapist is using skills that the client is not consciously aware of, tone of voice, observation, building rapport, leading, etc. They do not know techniques like free association or the fact that you are bypassing their conscious mind via a TDS; they don't need to know your skills. As long as the client understands what you are saying, they don't need to know the real reason you say certain things, or your body language like the manipulation anchor at the beginning of this script to get the client to say: "Conscious Mind." That skill used both verbal and non-verbal manipulation that the client is not aware of consciously. All they need to know is the understanding of their problem, how to solve the problem and understanding their own mind. What the therapist is doing in the back ground is a skill the client will never be fully conscious of. You the therapist are in fact controlling two minds very differently, yours and the clients and yours will be always one step ahead of the clients, because you have the psychotherapy skill knowledge that they don't. So there is no need to fully explain what you are in fact doing to the client, just make sure that what you are doing works.

What Do You Know About Hypnosis?

Dear student, only say the following if the client is worried about being hypnotised, because the more they understand, the more they will relax around the idea of being hypnotised, because their negative worrying preconceptions are wrong. Continue:

Well, I cannot make you do anything that you do not want to do. This surprises some people because they see those hypnosis shows on the TV and it does make it look like they are making people do what they do not want to. Think about it, why do people go to see those shows? They go to be entertained, to see people act stupid. So then, they ask for a volunteer. Now who is going to volunteer? So the hypnotist entertainer has all these people on stage and he starts deciding who will be the most entertaining, who is the biggest show off. The people in the audience might be thinking that he is looking for people that are hypnotisable, but he is not, because he knows that anyone is hypnotisable, so he is looking for the biggest show offs, the ones that want to be the centre of attention, the biggest exhibitionists. Now he has got it made, he is not making them do something they do not want to do; he is making them do what they already want to do. And that is great because that is exactly what we are doing today. I am not making you overcome your past problem; I am helping you do something you already want to do. Hypnosis is a great way for getting you to do what you already want to do but couldn't, due to trying consciously. When you relax via hypnosis you will not fall asleep, you will be aware of everything. You hear the sounds outside the room, the sounds from in the room, you remember everything. You still have thoughts running through your mind, one of those thoughts might be: "Am I hypnotised?" Well the answer to that is yes, because hypnosis is a feeling of being relaxed, and because you are relaxed, I can talk directly to the subconscious part of your mind in order to help you overcome the past problem.

The best way to describe hypnosis is to say that it feels like first thing in the morning, you have just woken up but you have not opened your eyes yet, you know you can open your eyes if you want to, but you do not want to because you are so relaxed. You are going in and out of hypnosis all day long, without even realising it. The most common form of hypnosis is driving. You are driving down the road on a trip you have done a hundred times before and you start to daydream or think about something else. Next thing you know you get to your destination and you have no idea how you got there. That is: "Highway Hypnosis." Whilst driving, your conscious mind has wandered off and your more powerful subconscious has driven you safely to your destination, due to the habit of driving the same route many times in the past. Also, reading a book or watching the TV. You are at home and you are watching TV and you are hanging on every word that is happening. Someone asks you a question and you do not hear them, or you do not want to hear them, because you are so relaxed and don't want to be disturbed.

Now there are a number of ways to respond to hypnotic suggestions. For example: you could respond within your mind by thinking: "Yes" or "No." So if I make a suggestion of: "You are now ready to overcome the past problem" and you think: "Yes I am" then that suggestion will work, and it will work every time in working towards a positive result of achieving your goal. Another way to respond is to be uncomfortable with the suggestion. For example: if I say: "You are now ready to confront your fear" and you think: "No I am not" then that suggestion I made will be rejected, so you are in control at all times. I sometimes have people in therapy who have been sent to me by their husbands, wives, or doctors, and they say: "Get in there and sort your problem out" and like I said, I cannot make someone do what they do not want to do. So again the suggestion is rejected because that type of client is unmotivated, they do not want to overcome their problem. Another way to respond is to hope. Now, there is a problem with the word hope, it is the twin sister of the word try. If I try to pick up this pen up, I do not do it because I am just trying, if I want to pick it up I will. The subconscious is too busy doing a hundred and one other things to care if you are just trying. Therefore if you are uncomfortable, unmotivated or just hoping and trying then the subconscious has not got time to listen and so will just reject any suggestions. However by being motivated and wanting change for the better, and by you agreeing and liking the suggestions I give, and by you wanting this session to work, not only will the positive suggestions be accepted, they will also be acted upon.

Hypnosis is like a contract between two people. My part of the contract is to give you all the thoughts and therapies that I know are going to make you happier. Your part of the contract is to follow along with the suggestions, want them to work and allow them to work. Now I know I am going to keep up with my part of the contract. Are you going to keep up to yours? Good, then we are going to be successful.

Dear student, at this point you can do a suggestion test on the client as explained in the Volume One Book. This will prove to them how powerful the subconscious mind is, it also adds to the belief in what you have told them about the mind model. Have you noticed that the information just given in this sub-chapter contradicts what I have taught you? With regards to what is said to the client when talking about hypnosis, I wrote: "Well, I cannot make you do anything that you do not want to do." As a student you know that is nonsense, because under hypnosis or light trace we can instruct a person to do anything. Even though that is true, the client doesn't need to know that, because they would feel uncomfortable around you, so what was said was simply giving them a deluded sense of control, when in fact they are not. It made them feel comfortable around hypnosis and therefore the session can continue.

Then I continue after the suggestibility test by saying: "Do you have any questions before you start living the life you want?"

Induce Hypnotic Trance

Dear student, remember when inducing trance within your client, you must pause when appropriate, in order to allow the client's mind to process what you are saying, and this also allows them time to respond. I am not going to write when to pause in this induction script because every induction is different, due to being personalised to the client. The feedback loop effect from observation is also important, monotone of voice and don't rush, simply talk slowly, in a relaxed manor, mirror their breathing at times, and personalise the trance from information from the pre-talk, all of which I have covered in detail in the Volume One Book. Continue:

As we begin you will take note of the different sounds in the room, the sound of my voice and thoughts or images that may drift through your mind and that is fine. It is now time to relax, please stare at the ceiling or light, take in a deep breath and relax as we release this breath. Continue breathing deeply and exhale slowly as you are learning to relax. As we continue here today, feeling peaceful, both you and I want to remain comfortable as you listen and concentrate on what I am saying, because what I say is important to you in achieving relaxation here today and your goal. Simply let go of all the tensions now and enjoy the feeling of being relaxed. Now you must remember, as we continue to breathe in deeply and exhale, that sometimes you can hear my voice, as you can now, and sometimes it may seem very quiet, and at times it does not matter if you cannot consciously hear my voice at all, because you cannot turn your ears off and therefore your subconscious mind will still be taking in everything that I say. You cannot turn your sense of taste, touch or smell off and you cannot turn your eyes off, you will simply closed your eyelids over them, because you cannot turn your senses off, you are always in control. Take in a deep long breath, and hold it, then in a moment breathe out, and as you do so, you are releasing all the tension from the past day, week, month and year, that you may have experienced. Now allow your head to stay where it is and start to look down, as if you are looking down at your feet, even if you cannot see them. In a moment I am going to turn on some relaxing music that is going to help you relax even more as we continue.

(Turn backing induction music on)

Allow any thoughts you may have to float into the distance, as you become more and more relaxed as time goes by. Your eyes are now becoming so tired that they simply close, and as they do, you feel even more relaxed. Allow yourself to go to (yawn so that the client can hear you because this creates sameness as if having the same experience), a sleep-like state, so that what I say will go deeper into your subconscious mind and this will prove to be one hundred percent successful for you, that feeling of relaxation is wonderful, and we both know how wonderful relaxation feels, as you drift deeper as we continue. You are going to relax into a level of relaxing that you have only ever imagined until now. The mind and body connections are very powerful and as we continue you concentrate on what I say, your mind takes in this information and your body reacts by drifting deeper and deeper into a sleep-like relaxed state. Every time you breathe in, you then breathe out all that past tension as it floats away into the distance; this guarantees your success here today. You are an intelligent person and I know this because you have understood everything that I have educated you with so far today; this also guarantees that you are able to achieve your goal from this moment forwards and you know you are now also achieving relaxation. It may happen slowly at first, each person is different and we all relax at different levels over different periods of time and that is fine. The beauty of this is that it is void of having to do anything, simply relax and let go naturally.

Deepening Trance via Staircase

Now going deeper into relaxation as we continue and you can still hear my voice, and in order to travel deeper into this wonderful sleep-like state, we are going to travel down, all the way down the staircase of relaxation within our powerful minds, this staircase consist of ten steps, see yourself right now at the top on stair ten. This staircase could be anywhere you want it to be, anywhere your imagination takes you, up in the clouds, in the park or anywhere you feel comfortable, like on the beach maybe or even in your own home, as long as you see yourself at the top, on the tenth step of the staircase of relaxation, then the location does not matter as long as you like the location. I am going to count down from ten to one, and as I do, you will imagine yourself stepping down each step with each number that I count down on the staircase of relaxation. For every step you take down, you will drift ten times deeper into relaxation, drifting deeper and deeper into a sleep-like state. And on ten, see yourself stepping, drifting, and floating down, all the way down to step nine going ten times deeper into relaxation with every step you take. Step nine drifting down with your whole body, sinking down, feeling heavier, and heavier as we step down to eight. And on eight, for every breath you breathe in and then out, you are exhaling all the past tensions as we allow you to drift deeper downwards into a sleep-like trance state. Stepping, floating down now to step seven, going ten times deeper into relaxation with every number counted down as we float downwards towards step six. And on six, every muscle in your body relaxing more, and more, getting heavier each and every time you breathe out, stepping down another step to number five. Continue to concentrate on my voice, allow yourself to let go because it feels so nice to relax more than you have for many years. And we continue to go down the staircase of relaxation to step four, feeling wonderful and enjoying this experience as it happens totally naturally, without any effort whatsoever. Step three now, see yourself floating down even further releasing all that past tension as we go, as you relax. In a moment we are going to reach the bottom of the staircase of relaxation, as we drift down to step two, and on one deeply relaxed, your whole body relaxed.

Continue by Deepening Trance Further via Bed Image

Now that we have drifted down the staircase of relaxation, and now at the bottom we can allow your body to relax even more, because I want you to imagine that there is a large comfortable double bed at the bottom of this staircase, where you are now. See yourself walking over to that warm comfortable bed, pulling the covers back and slowly climbing into that safe environment, lying down, pulling that warm blanket over you right now. And as you relax you take one last yawn,(once again yawn so that the client can hear you because this creates sameness as if having the same experience).And that sleep-like state feels warm and safe as we continue further into relaxation. Allow your mind to concentrate only on my voice at all times, as you enter that dreamlike state that feels so wonderful.

Continue by Deepening Trance Further via Body Parts

We are now ready to relax each and every area of your body, and we are going to start with your head area working downwards into relaxation. Each and every muscle in your forehead, right now relaxing, and your cheeks both cheeks relaxing, drifting down, feeling effortless as you continue to relax. Your jaw relaxing and eye lids are getting heavier and heavier, your whole face and head relaxing feeling sleepier, heavier, drifting down, and relaxing. Now moving down towards your neck area, relaxing, your head may drift to one side as you are becoming more and more tired and relaxed. Each and every muscle within your body is going deeper and deeper into a sleep-like state. You will enjoy this relaxed state as we continue, moving down, drifting down to your shoulders, both shoulders feeling limp as they relax even more, you now feel so lethargic, sinking down, feeling heavy as we move down both arms. Allowing them to go limp and drift downwards into a sleep-like state, sinking down into deep relaxation. Concentrate on your chest and stomach area, with each and every breath you breathe out you are sinking further and further down whilst enjoying the experience. Drifting down both arms, relaxing going limp and heavy towards both hands now, imagine all those muscles in each and every finger and both thumbs going limp, heavy and relaxed. (Add your observations of the client's hands and other body parts once mentioned.)

Feeling so tired and relaxed, it is so easy to achieve this relaxed state by simply allowing it to happen naturally and enjoying the relaxation as you breathe in and out relaxing more. Now from the top of your legs, as we work down to your knees achieving relaxation as you drift off feeling calm, safe, and warm. Downwards now, down both legs, relaxing down to your ankles. With every breath you take in, you then breathe out and sink even further down. Imagine your feet, allowing your toes to go limp, both feet limp, relaxed and heavy. All the way from the top of your head, all the way down to your feet, you are now deeply relaxed. And this feeling of relaxation continues as you concentrate on my voice, because what I say is very important to you, because it encourages your subconscious to remember that you are achieving relaxation, and by doing so you will also achieve your goal, for which you came here today.

Continue by Deepening Trance Further if Needed

We are now going to travel into a deeper state of relaxation from the count of ten moving down to one, and drifting ten times deeper, feeling more relaxed with every number heard being counted down. And on ten, drifting, and floating down, all the way down to a deeper state of trance. And on nine going ten times deeper into relaxation with every number being counted down, drifting down with your whole body, sinking down, feeling heavier, and heavier. And on eight, for every breath you breathe in and then out, you are exhaling all the past tensions away as you drift deeper downwards into a sleep-like trance state. Stepping, floating down now going deeper, going ten times deeper into relaxation with every number I count down, as you float downwards towards your desired goal and step seven, relaxing. And on six, every muscle in your body relaxing more and more, getting heavier with each and every breath, breathing out, drifting down towards number five. Continue to concentrate on my voice, allow yourself to let go because it feels so nice to relax more than you have for many years. We continue to count down to four, closer to the level of relaxation needed for success, feeling wonderful and enjoying this experience as it happens, totally naturally, without any effort whatsoever. Three now, I want you to see yourself floating down even further releasing all that past tension as we go, and relax. In a moment you are going to reach the desired level of relaxation as you drift down to number two, and on one deeply relaxed, your whole body relaxed.

Hypnotic Therapy Session Begins and Ends

Dear student, slightly up your tone from monotone to low volume normal speech, then continue:

As you sit, feeling drowsy and relaxed you continue to listen to my voice giving you all the positive suggestions that you require. As we continue you remain in the pleasant state of mind that you are now in. Remaining relaxed and peaceful, even drifting deeper as time goes by. Your whole body developing even further those deep, relaxing, warm feelings from the top of your head to your feet. We are now going to expand upon this new knowledge that you have required here today, making this a permanent part of your new way of thinking. The negative past will simply evaporate like a cloud on a summer's day and a new you will start to emerge for positive effect. My voice may seem to fade into the distance at times, and other times you are fully aware of what I say, this is totally normal as you drift between different levels of trance. Everything I say will seep deep into your subconscious mind, and remain there for your benefit, so that you can act upon the positive suggestions from this day forwards.

Pain or Pleasure Suggestion Techniques

Dear student, other different methods of pain or pleasure techniques will now be explained, that I didn't add in the weight loss script.

Obviously you will not be using them all in one session, one or two is enough, so adapt to suit your client's needs. Remember to always end a negative with a positive in order to always leave the client feeling positive. You can use the methods already shown or these ones that I will now explain.

Pain or Pleasure - Car Crash

Dear student, some clients are so stubborn in believing it is safe to smoke when driving, that I go to extremes to change their mind, so these clients must be pushed harder than other clients when leading them into an abreaction.

When I say: pushed, I mean you need to be harsher with them by showing them a truly devastating future image within their subconscious. They are the type of client that thinks they have one up on you as if they are right to smoke, they may smile and smirk at some of the things you have said in the pre-talk. This is the childlike mentality coming out due to not wanting to face what they have done to themselves and others. So, the only way to change this thought pattern is to create more neurological pain than normal. It is rare I need to push a client to the level I am going to show you, and again this takes great skill and confidence in your ability to judge the client's breaking point.

In order to continue my success with a client it is sometimes necessary to say the following:

"You have told me that you smoke when you drive and you think this is safe, so I want you to see yourself right now driving down the road and at some point you feel like smoking. See yourself driving along and at the same time searching for your cigarettes with one hand, having taken it off the steering wheel. You now have only one hand on the wheel and the other is searching for your cigarettes. At some point you look down and by doing so you have taken your eyes off the road to make it easier for you to find those cigarettes, because you think they are so important to you. But of course you have told me that this is safe as you take a cigarette out of the packet with either one or both hands, one holding the packet and the other pulling that cigarette out. Or you may hold the packet between your knees and use one hand to take the cigarette and place it into your mouth. Again, of course, you think this is safe as you travel thirty to seventy miles per hour. That cigarette is so important to you, as if your life depends on it. At no point have you considered the lives of other road users or pedestrians, due to your own selfish thoughts towards wanting that silly little white stick.

You then need to light the cigarette, so once again you go searching around but this time for your lighter. You have to once again take your eyes off the road whilst you light the white stick as you continue to drive. But again you have told me this is safe, but what the hell, you do not need to concentrate on the road at all times do you? You then start to smoke the cigarette holding it between two fingers, effectively disabling one hand from controlling your vehicle, and because you are holding the cigarette, only two fingers and a thumb are on the steering wheel because your other hand is changing gears when needed.

Do you think that if you had to make an emergency stop now, those two fingers and a thumb would effectively control your vehicle? Of course not, because the steering wheel would be ripped from your non-effective grip. Those few seconds is all it takes to lose control whilst travelling at speed. In order to take control of your vehicle whilst making an emergency stop to avoid something in the road, you would have to drop the burning cigarette on your lap making it an even more dangerous situation, those few seconds is all it takes to lose control. So see yourself right now driving along at thirty miles per hour smoking a cigarette. As you continue to drive along the road, suddenly without warning in front of you, your son David steps into the road, but that silly little white stick is more important to you, so you don't have full control of the steering wheel in order to veer out of his way to avoid hitting him. You continue to drive out of control in panic, as you drop the hot cigarette on to your lap, in order to attempt to take back control of the steering wheel with a full grip, but then, BANG!!! It's too late as it all happens so quickly, within seconds. You have hit your son David with the car"

Dear student, at this point make a loud bang verbally and by clapping your hands at the same time. I can assure you that your client will not awaken from trance, even so they may jump, and that is a good thing because it means they are truly submerged in the situation within their imaginative mind that you have placed them. Then continue:

"A second Bang! As David's body goes flying through the air hitting the windscreen, but of course that cigarette was far more important to you. You brake hard but it is too late! You stop the car and get out, finding your son dying in the road, all because that silly white stick was so important to you. Now that may not be your son lying there fighting for life, but it is someone's son, daughter, mother, father, brother or sister. Is that cigarette more important to you than a life? It must have been or you would not have selfishly been smoking it. It is now time to become that non-smoker and save your life, and that of your loved ones."

Pain or Pleasure - Drawing

"Imagine yourself sitting at home now, relaxing peacefully on your settee, and your son David comes over to you with a piece of paper and excitedly says: "Mummy I have drawn you a picture." How thoughtful of your son to have drawn you a picture. Every mother would love their son to have thought of them in that way. He hands over the drawing to you and you smile as you think to yourself what a lovely thought. You then look at the picture and it is a drawing of a wooden box with smoke coming out of it. Above the smoke your son has drawn an arrow pointing into the box and he has written, here lies my mummy, she died from smoking. The drawing is of you in a wooden coffin, having died from selfishly smoking, never once considering your son's feelings. It is your son's way of telling you that he loves you and he does not want you to die, he is begging you to stop smoking. You now know that it is time to stop smoking."

Dear student, this has actually happened to several of my clients, so now, for those clients with young children I factor this into some sessions, of course in a personal way to the client, using their child's name. Also many clients have told me that their children have downloaded pictures of smoke related diseases and they have given the pictures to them. It is a child's way of expressing love and their fear of the thought of losing their mummy or daddy to a smoke related death.

I can remember one client whose young son had been in his garden at home, and he witnessed his elderly neighbour being brought out of the house in a body bag. The young boy knew that his dead neighbour had been a heavy smoker so he shouted for his daddy and said to him: "Daddy I don't want you to die, please stop smoking." However that hadn't stopped him smoking until I made him relive the situation under hypnosis, which made the situation became real for him as it affected him on a subconscious level. He abreacted associating all the painful emotion to the anchor of smoking and he didn't smoke again.

Pain or Pleasure - Russian Roulette

"I want to tell you a story about a man, (or woman depending on the sex of your client.) This man has concerns of knowing whether smoking can really kill a person not, so he goes to his doctor to find out. On asking, the doctor replies: "The fact is one more cigarette could kill you, you could die within minutes of smoking one more cigarette." This worried the man (or woman but for this example I will use a man) thought, could one more cigarette really kill me? He wasn't sure so he makes appointments with five other doctors for their opinions to his question. The second doctor said: "Well it's unlikely if you are feeling ok within yourself but I'm not clear on the subject, I suppose it is possible you could die after one more cigarette." The remaining doctors said a similar thing.

Days later this man was sat at home thinking to himself that one doctor had said he could die by smoking one more cigarette and the other five were not certain, so he was confused by this, but with him being a smoker he decided to light up anyway. As he sat there smoking he turned the television on and the local news programme. The news reporter is talking about a man who, while playing Russian roulette, killed himself with a single shot to the head. He had a six shot revolver, placed just one bullet in it, spun the barrel, then took his chances and died.

The man smoking on his settee, watching this on television, thought how foolish of a man to do that, playing Russian roulette, giving himself one chance to die and five gambles on living. The realisation then came to the man whilst smoking, of his own situation, out of the six doctors that he had been to one had said he could die, and the other five were not sure. "One chance to die and five gambles on living." It was the same as playing Russian roulette with his life, the same as the man with the six shot revolver. (Client's name) have you ever played Russian roulette with your life? Gambling on whether you live or die? (Pause for a moment to give the client time to think). Well (Client's name) that is exactly what you have been doing with your life, you have been playing Russian roulette with your life where cigarettes are concerned, just the same as the man with the gun. At what point does your body tell you, "Enough is enough?" Because it can no longer cope with the poisonous chemicals that you have been abusing yourself with, and your chances to live are at an end. That's why you are here today, to stop smoking completely, to stop playing that silly game of Russian roulette with your life. I want you to realise that you have made it. You have become free of that old unwanted smoking habit in time to reverse any damages. By freeing yourself of that tobacco poison you are giving your body the ability to repair itself. By doing so, you will find yourself living a longer and healthier, happier life with more money in your pocket. Imagine yourself weeks from now, see yourself with your family and friends, you have a clean bill of health. You feel better than you have ever done in your life, and you are so glad that you became the non-smoker that you have become today. If you get withdrawal symptoms or cravings, you will remember that those feelings are only due to the past psychological addiction (psychological dependence) of the habit. Those feelings will be an enjoyable experience because they will serve as reminder of what you have achieved in becoming a non-smoker. In time the habit will no longer remind you because your subconscious realises you are a non-smoker, free from the bad destructive habit.

You have made one of the most important decisions of your life. You have decided to save your life, and possibly the lives of others by giving up smoking. Your lungs perform one of the most important functions in your body and without them you cannot breathe. It is essential for your health and your life to keep your lungs clean and fill them with fresh air. Your lungs have to cope with pollution in the air that you breathe, and your lungs can usually cope with that. But the strain of that extra concentrated pollution you were sucking in from each cigarette was weakening your mouth, your throat, your lungs, your stomach, and your blood was carrying choking smoke and poisonous toxins instead of the essential oxygen your body needs to fully function. Chemicals are sprayed on the tobacco as it grows, to kill insects, and many other chemicals, up to four thousand in fact, and they have been slowly killing you. You had been forcing people around you, people who you believe you love, even your children, but yet you were forcing them to breathe in those foul toxins in the past. Now, you choose to reject tobacco and its foul toxins and develop a new habit, a clean and pleasant habit, that of being a non-smoker. Just as you taught yourself to smoke, you have now decided to teach yourself a new and much better habit, that of being free from tobacco and its deadly toxins."

Pain or Pleasure - Large Container Image

"Imagine a large container at the side of you now. This container holds all the tar and poisons from cigarettes that you have smoked over the last (number of years that the client has smoked). All this tar and poisons are compacted within this container, making it the size of an average settee or chair similar to the one you are relaxing on now. You are connected to this container because it is part of you and it has been for many, many years. It is attached via an umbilical cord from your lungs, and you carry this burden around with you wherever you go. As you look inside this container, you can see all those deadly, cancerous poisons that you have consumed over the years. This is something to be truly ashamed off because all your loved ones are also carrying a shameful container around with them, due to all the cigarettes you have poisoned them with. Your loved ones do not have a choice other than to carry this poison around with them, as you selfishly over many years poisoned them. You wrongly thought that you needed that poison, the burden on your life, when in fact you now realise that you are ready to cut the poison from your life and by doing so, your loved ones burden of carrying a container around with them will also be gone as well, and as a result everyone's health will improve, including yours. At the moment this disgusting burden is still attached to you and your loved ones and it follows you, no matter how you try to deny it with all those excuses that you have told me, it still follows you. Everyone you know and even people that you don't know can smell this embarrassing poison on you as you carry it around with you, but of course you have thought that you need this shame hanging around with you all the time, day in and day out. It is controlling your life instead of you being in control of it. It is now time to take back control; this is your time, here and now to say, "Enough is enough; I want to be free of that burden, of that unhygienic smell and cancerous poisons." Now within your mind I want you to cut that umbilical cord, therefore cutting yourself free from that past burden and also releasing your loved ones from theirs as well that you caused. Push that container away because you are now free. Once you have done that send me a sign by rising up one of your fingers on your right hand. Feels good doesn't it? Well done, we are doing fantastic. Now your health can recover over the next days and weeks and coming years."

Pain or Pleasure - Death, Pain and Sorrow

"You have made a positive, life changing decision today, and this is to be the non-smoker that you are now. From this day forwards when you see someone smoking or you smell cancerous cigarette smoke, you will instantly think of the words: "Death, Pain and Sorrow." You will pity the person that is smoking as you think of the words: "Death, Pain and Sorrow." But you cannot help them. They can only seek help themselves, as you have done today. "Death, Pain and Sorrow." You will think of those words because you are an intelligent person and you know that all a cancerous cigarette will ever bring into anyone's life is: "Death, Pain and Sorrow." Death to the person that is smoking, and pain, and sorrow to the loved ones that remain in this world, the ones that are forced to go to the smoker's funeral after watching them die slowly. I say forced because given the option they would rather have their loved one still alive, but due to selfish reasons the death came, and pain, and sorrow followed.

Every time you see someone smoking or you smell cancerous cigarette smoke, you will instantly think of the words "Death, Pain and Sorrow" and you will pity the person that is smoking as you think of the words: "Death, Pain and Sorrow." This: "Death, Pain and Sorrow" could be caused by you, if you ever have a weak, selfish moment and attempt to smoke yourself to: "Death, Pain and Sorrow." "Death, Pain and Sorrow" will enter your mind every time you see, touch or smell a cigarette and you will never taste one again. Because all that a cancerous cigarette will ever bring to you is: "Death, Pain and Sorrow" and you will be reminded of this if you ever so much as touch a cancerous cigarette. The thought of you smoking repulses you, as it does most people. You will also remember all of the reasons that you have become a non-smoker today, to live, and enjoy life in a fit and healthy body, for yourself and your loved ones. What an amazing achievement that has been made to be so easy for you, now that you fully understand the habit and your mind."☐

Pain or Pleasure - Image of One's Self

"Let us imagine now that the person that you once were, the smoker, is sitting next to you right now. I want you to watch the person that you once were smoking at the side of you now. (Client's name) we are working together today to make sure you remain to be the non-smoker that you have become here today, however I want you within your mind to see that past smoker at the side of you right now smoking. As you witness yourself smoking, you may think, what on earth was I doing? You can see all those chemicals entering the face and hair within the smoke. You can see how foolish this past person that you once were, how daft you once looked when smoking. See that cigarette in the lips, sucking on it; breathing in all those poisons, you were killing yourself slowly over a period of many years. Twenty to thirty times a day playing Russian roulette with your life, see yourself right now smoking. How does it make you feel seeing yourself smoking? (Pause giving the client time to think) Horrified? Ashamed? Wishing you had never smoked, wishing you had a second chance in life? The person that you once were, that selfish smoker, was limiting your pleasures in life, wasting hours a day of your life smoking, taking away your money, your health, and several years off your life span, everything to do with smoking is so negative, so destructive, so devastating. You remember those words: "Death, Pain, and Sorrow." They remind you of how lucky you are to have this second chance in life, to live in a healthy body for a good quality of life. You are now ready to move forwards in your life for the greater good of your family and yourself, push that old image of you smoking away, and be grateful this second chance of life has come your way. Even so, remember to never delude yourself that you have a third chance in life because you won't, this is your second chance for positive change and you will never get a third chance. So embrace this new beginning, imagine yourself years in the future, continuing to have good health as a non-smoker and enjoying life in a fit and healthy body. Would you ever want to be that smoker ever again? No, so once again push that image away and congratulations on your achievements today. Feels great to be alive doesn't it? Being a non-smoker, and knowing that you are going to be in this world a lot longer for your loved ones. Be proud of yourself for making the leap forwards and taking back control of your life."

Creative Visualisation of Removing the Past

"(Client's name) remain where you are now, sat peacefully feeling calm, and in front of you, within your imagination you are to imagine a television that is turned on with a movie of you in it. This movie is an old film of you smoking. Watch this movie from the past, as you once were for all those years. See yourself smoking, self-abusing yourself, making you more, and more miserable as time went by, as your health suffers. It is time to remove the past once and for all, and in order to achieve this goal you need to destroy the negative past. Having seen the past you want to remove it and so you are more than happy, and willing to destroy this past image. This television holds the bad habit and all the memories associated to it. In order to remove this bad habit from your life, you need to turn the volume control all the way down to zero so that the past bad habit can no longer be heard. Do that now within your powerful subconscious mind, and you also need to turn the contrast and colour all the way down so that the old negative image of you can no longer be seen or heard.

Even so the memory of the past problem is still in the television set, so it is very important that it is destroyed, once and for all, forever. So you now need to turn the power supply off to the television, which detaches the past, making it possible to move forwards in your life. Turn the power off to the television now which turns your past off. In order to make sure the negative past person, whom you once were has gone, you also need to pick up an imagined hammer and hit the television with all your force and power, continuing in hitting it until it is hundreds of pieces.

How you once acted and what you once did, abusing yourself with smoking, that person from your past has now been removed, so you can now move forwards in life feeling proud and healthy. It feels so good to have gotten rid of that past negative person doesn't it? Send me a sign again by raising up a finger on the right hand to show me you have finished destroying the past negativity and it feels good. (Wait for the sign) we can now continue with the session, and that's fantastic."

Improve Confidence Relevant to the Session Type, via a Thermometer to 100% Successful

The following can be said to your client:

Now (client's name), imagine a thermometer filled with water, you know what a thermometer looks like and this one has water within it that you can see through the clear glass of the thermometer. It has the numbers one to one hundred percent written on the glass of the thermometer from the bottom to one hundred percent being at the top. This thermometer represents your confidence level from feelings in the past towards your past low confidence etc. It may be set at ten percent at the moment; even so we need to achieve a level of one hundred percent for this session to be successful. So let's imagine heating up the water that is within the thermometer with a flame thrower. The water lever is at ten percent at the moment, making your confidence level ten percent, however by heating up the thermometer the percentage level will rise as the water heats up and therefore your confidence level will rise also. By heating up the water your confidence level starts to rise up and up, making your confidence level improve, and rapidly rising 20% 30% 40%. See the level of your confidence rise as you heat up the thermometer with the flamethrower, moving the level up higher and higher, improving your confidence level, and as it does move upwards it is getting closer to one hundred percent, you feel even more confident as the water level and confidence rises. Once the desired level of one hundred percent has been achieved, I want you to send me a sign to confirm that this confidence thermometer is at one hundred percent by raising a finger on the right hand upwards, this indicates to me that we can move on to the next part of this technique. (Wait for the signal then move on). Turn the brightness up in your mind so that you can clearly see the improved overall confidence level, and considering this thermometer is filled with water, and that water is now at one hundred percent representing your achievement made here today, it needs to remain there at one hundred percent. To do this we need to place the thermometer into the fridge freezer. See yourself now; picking up the thermometer and walking over to the freezer, opening the door and placing your confidence level of one hundred percent within the freezer, your confidence level is now frozen forever at one hundred percent and it will remain there forever because it is now frozen. Fantastic, feels good because you have achieved a lot within this session, and you have overcome your past problem, so that your new positive life can start today.

Creative Visualisation of Future Image and More

"Now that the past smoker has been removed, it is time to see yourself as the new you that you have become today, the happier, more relaxed non-smoker, and you continue to be this person in the future, having changed today. Within your mind look into a full length mirror now and the reflection is that of what you are going to look and feel like a few weeks from now, once your body and health has recovered from all those years of self-abuse. That is fantastic, look how good you now look as you see this future reality of an image of your happier self. Your skin tone has improved, health in general, and you look amazing, healthier and happier with more energy. Friends have been commenting on how amazing you look and congratulating you on your achievement of becoming a non-smoker, you feel amazing. This reflection in the mirror is the person you have become because the process of change has already taken place within this session. This reflection is the person that you have always wanted to be, see yourself now stepping into this mirror, into your future self. You are to feel and see yourself now as the person you have always wished for, because this is now who you are, a non-smoker, and over the following weeks you will become more, and more like your true slim, fit, healthy self. Your friends will now say: (client's name) you look amazing, they will compliment you and you will feel the pride of achieving your goal. However should you ever experiment or try a cigarette for any excuse or reason, the moment you put a cigarette, or tobacco, to your lips, the moment you inhale you will feel nauseated to your core, you will feel sicker, physically sicker, than you have ever felt in your entire life. But the moment you let go of that cigarette, throw it away, then those feelings of sickness will leave you as quickly as (click fingers) that. You will instantly be filled with a sense of pride for saying: "Death, Pain and Sorrow" because that is all that cigarettes will ever cause you. But again, if under any circumstances you ever try to inhale a cigarette, it will taste disgusting, making you sick to your core, and those feelings will remain until you throw the cigarette away or put it out. The smell of other people's smoking will never, ever make you feel sick. However it is only, and I repeat only, if you ever try to smoke tobacco of any form, yourself, then, and only then, you will feel physically sick to your core, because you really hate it. But the very moment you throw that cigarette away, then those feelings of nausea will leave you instantly as quick as that (fingers snapping or clicking). ☐

You now feel better than you have ever done before. That feeling of pride has filled you up as well as the feelings of confidence and happiness. Each and every time someone says do you want a cigarette (name) you will be so happy when you say: "No, I am a non-smoker." See that now, in your mind's eye, saying: "No, I am a non-smoker" and notice how good it feels, and notice how proud you feel, how confident you feel. And most of all, notice how much healthier you feel. Because this is your reality now, knowing you are healthier and in effect you have added on years to your life by being 100% successful, by completing our work here today, so you are now ready to begin your new life as a non-smoker. Notice how good it feels to have taken back control from that silly, white cancerous stick. And know that you no longer want, need, crave, or desire cigarettes in any way shape or form. From this moment forward, if you ever touch a cigarette, the words: "Death, Pain and Sorrow" will enter your mind and each and every time, should you touch a cigarette the word: "Chemicals" will be clearly visible on the tip of the cigarette, within your imagination. Reminding you of all the deadly chemicals and poisons contained in each and every cigarette, reminding you of the hundreds of good reasons to stop killing yourself with self-abuse, and the people around you, and the ones you love. You are now a confident, happy, healthy, non-smoker. With an inner reservoir of willpower that you can and will draw upon whenever needed, because from this day forward, you are a successful, healthy non-smoker. It is you that has made the powerful lifesaving decision to stop smoking from this moment forwards, and because of this decision, together we have achieved this goal here today."

Associating Good Feeling to an Anchor

I now want to remember the memory of a time when you felt really good about yourself, we talked about this in the pre-talk when you were telling be about (use information from pre-talk and talk in an excitable positive tone), you feel really happy in that time so see yourself their now, relive it. And when you have that happy, emotional feeling from that past time, I want you to expand upon it, see the situation that you are in, and that wonderful feeling that is generated within you. The content details of the memory are not that important. What is important now for you are the emotional, happy feelings that the memory generates within you. (Personalise from information previously given from the pre-talk.)

I want you to really remember how you felt inside, those good, positive feelings, and strong feelings, confident and self-assured feelings and the laughter from that time. You can allow those good feelings to grow stronger and more positive whilst you take in a really long, deep breath, in through your nose, and now let's associate that good feeling to pressing together your thumb and the forefinger of the right hand, and by doing so you are making the ring of confidence, so that you are associating that good feeling to making the ring of confidence with your thumb and the forefinger which becomes the anchor. This is an associated emotion to an anchor, when we experience two things together for a little while, one will automatically remind us of the other, and repetition is the mother of success, so keep repeating this exercise over the following days and weeks, so that you are making the anchor of the ring of confidence with your finger and thumb into a signal to your subconscious mind to make you feel good, because that is the happy emotion that is now associated to the ring of confidence. So whenever you take in a really long deep breath through your nose and press together your thumb and the forefinger of the right hand, you are going to feel those good, strong, confident happy feelings once again, and you can feel these good feelings anytime you wish, anywhere, in any situation. Because these good, strong, confident feelings are becoming more and more a part of you and you are becoming that stronger, more confident person that will guarantee your success in achieving your goal of overcoming (whatever the problem was). And remember, anytime you want to feel even more confident, all you need to do is breathe in that really long, deep breath through your nose and press together the thumb and the forefinger of the right hand, and you will once again feel those good, strong, confident feelings filling your whole body in order to make you feel better and better. You can feel wonderful, calmer, more relaxed and much more confident than ever before. You know what it's like to feel those good, strong, confident feelings and you can really enjoy remembering and experiencing those feelings once again, which are becoming more and more a permanent part of you. Feels good doesn't it (suggested command and not a question). Send me a sign that it feels good by raising your right hand (this was using the anchor from pre-talk triggering the right answer). Of course it does because you just created a new more positive reality for yourself, and simply relax and put your right hand down now and that's fantastic. Work on generating good feeling and then press together the thumb and the forefinger over the next few days to reinforce the anchor trigger of good feeling, and see how real that associated anchor triggers the good feeling that can be used in the future whenever you need it. Any time in the future should you have a silly thought towards a past negative problem, simply do as you just have and feel good by saying no to the silly old problem, or use the anchor when in a bad situation to make you feel good, however right now, you can relax and let go of the ring of confidence, because it is not needed at this moment in time.

Post Hypnotic Suggestion

"It is now very helpful and pleasant to go back to the good feeling anchor that we created earlier, by making the ring of confidence once again with your finger and thumb. Make the ring of confidence now, see yourself right now in that time once again, and feel how good it does now, as it did back then. We have improved your overall way of thinking here today for positive effect from now and in the continued future. You know that you can use this ring of confidence whenever you chose to, making you feel relaxed and calm around any situation, that in the past you had a silly thought towards smoking. This wonderful feeling of being relaxed and comfortable is a simple state of mind that you can enter whenever you choose to as we have proven here today, you now know that you can relax more than you have in many years. You have now placed yourself in a positive reality and that old reality has now gone forever, this is due to your new understanding of yourself and the past problem that has made your goal easy to achieve. Your goal of becoming a non-smoker has been achieved here today and you can now move on with your life, free from that past, negative, bad habit self-abuse problem. All this new knowledge that you have learned here today has been stored within your subconscious mind, and the new information can and will be used whenever you need a reminder to help you through situations that you may find yourself in. All the suggestions your mind has taken in today are for the greater good for you and the people around you. You will act upon the suggestions you have received because you now know how to succeed, and you know you have, and you are continuing to succeed from this day forwards.

We have proven today that you can relax, without the silly thought of a white, cancerous stick, and this is an amazing achievement and a new beginning for you because you can achieve this same success each day. You have learned how powerful your subconscious mind is and you know that by focusing on positive imagined thoughts, brings about whatever it is you focused on, in this case, relaxation, so well done. Now that you have achieved what you have today, just think what else you can achieve and go and do it. You are looking forward to doing new things with all the money that you will now save from not poisoning yourself. You are motivated to achieve even more in life, whatever you want in life, going to the gym maybe or whatever it maybe. Over the weekend you will take your children (grandchildren, husband etc) for a walk in the country, it will be fun and enjoyable and whilst enjoying yourself you are simply recovering your lungs and health in general in the process.

If ever a silly craving enters your mind, your mind will revert back to that devastating image of (which ever pain technique image you use), and you will remember that a craving is a simple reminder that you have won in achieving your goal of being a non-smoker, because it means you are not smoking, so well done (name of client). All cravings are just your mind reminding you of a past habit, so enjoy the feeling, because it means you are a success and you continue to be. When you get home you will immediately throw away any cigarettes and ashtrays you have in your home because you are now a non-smoker and therefore your home is a smoke and nicotine free zone. You are a non-smoker and you will remain to be in the future forever, because you know that in order to be healthy and live longer, you need to remain the non-smoker that you now are. I am going to give you a hypnotherapy audio CD that you will take home because it will help you relax, the same as you now are doing here today. You will play it once every day, from today when you have a moment to yourself, or even in bed tonight and each night. Work on the good feeling anchor every day in the future for the next thirty days so that it becomes a permanent positive part of you."

End Session by Waking the Client from Trance

"After the count from one to ten, you are going to awaken. This process will be slow, giving you time to come around into a fully conscious state in your own time. Once fully conscious you will be so grateful and relieved that your past problem has gone. You will also realise the amazing, positive change within yourself, because this has been a positive life changing experience for you. You have not been able to relax for years but yet you have come here today to a total stranger's home, and done what you thought impossible, relaxed. What you have achieved today is amazing; in many respects it has been a revelation for you. It has been achieved by a simple change in your though processes, it is a state of mind that will now remain with you for life, for continued success."

And 1 – All the suggestions I have given you today will remain with you for life because you know how beneficial they are to you.
And 2 – From this day and every day in the future, this new beginning for you will fill you with joy of achieving your goal here today.
And 3 – Every morning you will be so happy to have this new beginning free from your past problem.
And 4 – Each day that passes you will get stronger and stronger as that past problem disappears into the distance, gone forever.
And 5 – Remembering to work on that good feeling anchor that we have created for positive effect today.
And 6 – All this new knowledge you now have, you can and will adapt it within all aspects of your life.
And 7 – Today you have been able to relax more than you have for many years, proving that you can achieve anything once you focus your mind on your goal.
And 8 – Each and every area of your body feeling refreshed and revitalised, ready to start your new way of life.
And 9 – In your own time, when you feel ready, simply open your eyes remembering all that has been said today.
And 10 – Fully awake now feeling amazing.

Dear student, Give the client a hypnotherapy relaxation CD and tell them they must listen to it every day, or night, as a booster to the session for at least thirty days for added support. This also helps them to work on the anchoring technique.

What to Expect after a Stop Smoking Session

What to expect after the session. About 30% of people after the session feel as if they have never had a cigarette in their lives. They never even think about it, although you have no way of knowing that until days after a session. Another 30+% will feel great, they have no cravings, but a week or so may go by and they might be getting in their car or talking on the phone and they have the odd thought about a cigarette. As fast as the thought enters their mind it'll be gone and they'll go about their business as a non-smoker. The last 30+% are people that might be sitting there with a cup of tea or coffee and have a little mind game with themselves, "I'd really like to have a cigarette, yes, no, yes, no." But as long as they remember to say: no, they'll be fine, and stand up and move around a bit to occupy their mind on a different stimulus. This leaves us with about 5% of people that every now and then, will come to me even though they really don't want to, they don't want to stop smoking because their husbands, wives, lovers, doctors or whoever pushed them in and said: "Get in there and make him make you a non-smoker." Well, because they don't want to stop smoking, long-term they won't, so nothing I say or do will work until they decide for themselves to stop smoking. Remember that those that want to stop smoking, we are helping them to do what they wanted to do, but they couldn't without help, and we make it easy for them, but those that don't want to stop won't. In all professions, you will get a small percentage of time wasters; this is the 5% that fail. I can remember one client that had no intensions of stopping smoking but yet he still stopped. However he was annoyed about it, so weeks later he started smoking again, but he couldn't go back to smoking the same number each day that he used to. He had in fact halved the number of cigarettes that he once smoked and this was a man that didn't want to stop, so think what you can achieve with clients that do want to stop. This same client was annoyed that he had been hypnotised because he did not believe it was possible. He could not understand how he had lost one hour of his time because he refused to accept it, he thought I had tampered with his watch, so he phoned a friend of his to ask them what time was it.

Your Journey Continues as this Book Ends

DEAR STUDENT, our journey together is close to completion. However the journey never ends, because life is a journey and not a destination, and the same can be said for your growing knowledge. If anyone ever says they know it all, about any subject, then they are very wrong, because there is always more to learn. After years of experience, it took me a further three years to write the first edition of my book: "Beginner to Advanced Practitioner Training Course & Self Development in Psychotherapy - Hypnotherapy - Neuro-Linguistic Programming (NLP) - Cognitive Behavioural Therapy (CBT) Clinical Psychology Vol: 1". Ten years later I am still adding more information, as I also continue to learn from experience, and I continue to share it with you.

I have written four script books. Those being: Phobia - Confidence & Anxiety - Weight Loss – Stop Smoking. You may want to invest in those script books as well.

You may be interested to know that I am working on a series of follow-up books to compliment my "Beginners to Advanced Volume One Book". The next book, which is the second volume, is very different than the first. Allow me to explain:
The entire client examples in all the script books, and in volume one are real, although what I have not done here, or in the first volume book, is write word for word, from beginning to the end, the dialog from full sessions of what my clients and myself have said. Instead, I wrote small sections of sessions from my experiences, to explain techniques to you and how clients think. I also wrote scripts to give you different ideas of what can be said. One of those books you have just read. The scripts were written in a way not intended to be read out to the clients word for word. I simply wanted to show you different, basic beginners and advanced ways of conducting therapy, in a structured session that you can personalise to each client.
In the next series of books starting from volume two onwards, I have written in full detail what is said from recordings that I have made of real client sessions. So the follow-up series, of books, are client case studies with each book being a different client case. In those books I will explain

in detail the techniques I am using and why I have said certain things to the client, and I will explain the client's reactions. The client case study sessions were conducted at an advanced level, because that is how I conduct sessions, and therefore those books are for students that have already read volume one, and not just a scripts.

For those wishing to buy the CD's that are mentioned in this book, they are available on one CD Rom for your computer and it has eleven audio hypnotherapy Mp3's with free copyright. This allows you to make copies on CD to sell to your clients to maximise your profits and to help the clients further. They focus on: Stopping Smoking, Losing Weight, Boosting Confidence, Stress Relief, Improving Study Habits, Focus of Concentration, and Pre-talk. Also an induction backing track with subliminal messages of relaxation is on the CD, and that you can play in the back ground as you hypnotise your client.

Simply go to: www.inspiredhypnotherapy.com and then click on the: 'Prices & Online Store' page. You can also contact me through the web site if you wish to have personal training from me.

For those students that have studied this book as a Home Study Course, if you wish to take the Diploma exam, then the option to do so is available as shown on my web site: www.InspiredHypnotherapy.com on the page: "Prices & Online Store". The exam is done in your own free time from the comfort of your own home. You simply email me your answers. Students that pass will receive a Diploma Certificate, as shown on the web site.

Please add me on Facebook – 'David Glenn - Psychotherapy NLP CBT Hypnotherapy'. I am building a community of like-minded people, including my past students. I will post information on my new published books, and we can all help one another with questions and answers regarding psychotherapy as a whole.

Dear student, if you have any questions you want answering to further your knowledge, or you simply want to talk, then please phone me. Phone calls are free via Wi-Fi on WhatsApp from anywhere in the World. Telephone 07973481786

Of course I have to charge for my time. Those charges being £25 for half hour or less. Or £45 for over half an hour to an hour. We can cover many topics in that time. Payment must be made online before the call is made in order to schedule a time and date for our conversation.

I also conduct therapy sessions over the phone if you, or someone you know can't travel to see me in person at the same cost.

Simply email me your details, how much of my time you wish to have, dates and UK times that you are free to talk, and I shall email you a request for payment and set scheduled session. Alternatively in person I charge £95 for a full one and a half hour session.

david.glenn.psychotherapy@gmail.com

Dear student. Can I please ask for a few moments of your time to leave positive feedback on the site where you invested in this book? Without feedback, my time writing will have been wasted, because few people will invest in the book and I simply want to help people to study, to help others, and also for people to overcome their personal psychological problems.

Please note that I am not a professional writer. I am a therapist. Even so, I have done my best to write this book to help others and you. So please excuse the odd grammar error or spelling mistake. This book has been written in UK English and not American-English and for that reason many words are spelt differently to what our American friends are used to.

Thank you!

Dear student, I wish you all the happiness in the world and good health, until our paths cross again in 'Volume One or Two or more' or another script book. Bye for now.

Printed in Great Britain
by Amazon